"Robert Jackman's *Healing Your Lost Inner Child* is a rare find among the tens of thousands of self-help books. Jackman brilliantly communicates his original ideas, concepts, and clinical direction while staying true to cutting-edge information on the subject of trauma resolution. Those suffering from attachment trauma will feel enveloped by Jackman's authentic and highly relatable passion for this subject. Readers will be forever transformed by his understanding of complex trauma and his coherent instruction on how to solve it. This brilliant book instills optimism and courage to dig deep into the shame-stained areas of your life, so that you can heal."

—Ross Rosenberg, MEd, LCPC, CADC, CSAT Psychotherapist,
author of *The Human Magnet Syndrome: The Codependent Narcissist Trap*, and creator of the Codependency Cure™ Treatment Program

"*Healing Your Lost Inner Child* is a beautiful, accessible book written by a highly empathic and compassionate therapist. It flows seamlessly from beginning to end and, despite its depth, is easy to read. In his own unique, artistic way, Robert Jackman weaves his hard-won practical wisdom into the book in a helpful, concrete, and grounded way, using his own painful experiences to help others transform theirs. As I read it, I could feel the unhealed pieces of me that needed to receive it gently opening up to absorb its wisdom. Your inner child will thank you for reading this book."

—Stacy Dicker, PhD, Psychologist and author of *Psychstrology: Apply the Wisdom of the Cosmos to Gain Balance and Improve Your Relationships*

"Robert Jackman is a profoundly insightful and dedicated healer with many years of experience. In *Healing Your Lost Inner Child*, he has distilled underlying truths of what exists in each of us and how those truths affect our outlook on life and behavior with others. He gives us a way to find insight based on our personal history, then guides us in developing tools to foster a deep satisfaction and greater happiness for ourselves and our loved ones. It is a wonderful feeling to use the HEAL process to work through the complex maze of one's past and find the way to understanding, forgiveness, and well-being. Whether you are lucky enough to be (partially) healed or are still embroiled in toxic drama, there is deep wisdom in this book."

—David Brumwell, MD

"This masterpiece allows the reader to develop self-awareness in order to reach deep down, heal, and awaken into a new being. We all have our own inner guides that help us grow. Robert Jackman brings out the strengths that we already have in healing the lost part of ourselves."

—Jamie Kruse, MSW, LCSW (Trauma Therapist)

"If you make the time to work through Robert Jackman's *Healing Your Lost Inner Child* and the HEAL process, I am confident you will see profound results. This is a clear, compassionate, and effective guide to healing and thriving written by a master therapist. This book can be used as a blueprint to create an internal and external relational balance that can bring real joy. I highly recommend this gentle yet direct, trauma-informed guide to anyone looking to do the sometimes uncomfortable work of deep healing. It will be an essential resource for therapists and clients alike. The exercises alone are worth much, much more than the cost of the book."

—Scott Conklin, MFA, LCPC

"In *Healing Your Lost Inner Child*, Robert Jackman provides empathetic, step-by-step encouragement for anyone who has ever asked, 'Why do I always do that?' Using nonjudgmental language, he gives multiple examples of real people struggling to identify the source of their childhood wounds and the boundaries they have created to protect from, and cope with, triggering events in adulthood. Identifying and healing past wounds, developing comfortable and safe boundaries for the future, and embracing an authentic life are goals toward which we all should strive. Jackman has provided us with an excellent road map for our journey."

—Karen L Hawkins, Attorney at Law, JD, LLB (honorary), MBA, Former Director, Office of Professional Responsibility, Internal Revenue Service, United States Treasury Department

"In *Healing Your Lost Inner Child*, Robert Jackman has created a comprehensive resource for therapists and those who want to heal inner wounds. Through research, stories, and case examples, Jackman helps the reader who seeks wholeness to move forward from wounds of childhood. I imagine the world will be better because of this book, as we all need to heal our lost inner child. I highly recommend this book to therapists and anyone who wishes to feel lighter."

—Joe Sanok, Podcaster and Licensed Counselor,
creator of Practice of the Practice

"If you've found yourself stuck in the same patterns of sadness, anger, or fear, or if you're reliving the same relationship pain over and over, *Healing Your Lost Inner Child* is for you. Robert Jackman has created a beautiful and detailed roadmap for identifying and healing the internal dynamics that impact our repetitive and painful life patterns. It is highly accessible, user- friendly, and full of heart and hard-earned wisdom. Jackman walks us through focused exercises, and uses examples from his personal life and from case studies to bring clarity to the confusion. Inspiring and a delight to read."

—Mark Pletcher, MA, LCPC Psychotherapist and Relationship Coach

"*Healing Your Lost Inner Child* truly captures the essence and elegance of the HEAL process. Those who are committed to self-healing will find the stories relevant and the exercises enlightening."

— Joel J. Hass, MD, Family Practice Physician, Nantucket, MA

HEALING
Your Lost
Inner Child

HEALING
Your Lost
Inner Child

How to Stop Impulsive Reactions,
Set Healthy Boundaries and
Embrace an Authentic Life

ROBERT JACKMAN
MS, LCPC, NCC

 PRACTICAL WISDOM PRESS

Healing Your Lost Inner Child: How to Stop Impulsive Reactions, Set Healthy Boundaries and Embrace an Authentic Life

Copyright © 2020 by Robert Jackman, LCPC

ISBN (paperback): 978-1-7354445-0-5
ISBN (ebook): 978-1-7354445-1-2

Published by Practical Wisdom Press
www.theartofpracticalwisdom.com

Edited by Jessica Vineyard, Red Letter Editing, LLC, www.redletterediting.com
Book Design by Christy Collins, Constellation Book Services

Printed in the United States of America

To my parents, Rose Mary and Bob Jackman

Contents

Acknowledgments

To my late parents, Rose Mary and Bob Jackman, thank you for always believing in me and for filling and expanding my heart with your love. Deep within, I carry the solid foundation of family, love, and believing in myself that you both established. Thank you for always encouraging me to follow my dreams and to go for it. I miss your presence on Earth every day.

To my sister, Cindy Van Liere, thank you for always being there for me, for your spark of life and the brightness you bring to the world. Thank you for being so much more than just my sister; you are my friend. Every day in so many ways you make me proud to be your big brother. I can't imagine my life without you in it. You are a beautiful person inside and out. I love you.

To my love, Drew Caldwell, thank you for your kindness and sweet, loving, committed energy over the last thirty years. Thank you for always thinking I'm incredible and can do anything I set my mind to. Thank you for your grace and compassion when my woundings showed up. I wouldn't be the man I am today without you, and I can't imagine sharing this journey with anyone else. I love you.

Thank you to all those over the course of my career who have come to me professionally and shared the story of your inner child. My consciousness expands, learns, and is enriched by each of you, and for that I am humbly grateful.

To all of my friends who listened to me go on and on about the book I was writing and who gave me unlimited encouragement and love, thank you.

To my brothers in Victories for Men, your authentic expressions helped to create a safe place for me to reveal and discover more about myself. In 2008 I started searching to know myself better and to find more ways to heal my woundings. I started attending Victories for Men weekend retreats, where I met other men who were searching how to heal their wounded inner child. I was able to see men being courageous and vulnerable, open-hearted and compassionate. Not only did I meet other like-minded men and develop deep friendships, I also learned how to demonstrate healthy masculinity. I repaired big parts of my distorted worldview of what it means to be a man, and worked on my childhood wounding so that I could fully embrace my authentic self. Thank you, brothers. Victoriesformen.org

To my mentor Kristin Armstrong, who taught me the value of creating a strong boundary system in order to have a fulfilling life, and that self-love can be found in our wounded past. Your wise counsel over the years has helped me more than you know. Thank you for being my friend.

Thank you to my other mentor, the late Rev. Don Burt, who taught me that "families are places where people are made" and to remember that I am a spiritual being having a human experience.

A special acknowledgment goes to the way-showers and thought leaders in the fields of psychology, philosophy, and spirituality who have influenced my own healing as well as my work in creating the HEAL process. I stand on the shoulders of these giants.

Thank you to the late John Bradshaw, author of *Homecoming: Reclaiming and Championing Your Inner Child.* Twenty years ago I went to a weekend retreat where John Bradshaw and Claudia Black took us through his process, and I learned how to connect even deeper with my inner child. I credit John Bradshaw with helping me understand the deep healing that can come about through writing to the inner child and how its integration with the adult self is key to the entire process.

Thank you to Pia Mellody, author of *Facing Codependence: What It Is, Where It Comes From, How It Sabotages Our Lives*, for her groundbreaking work in the field of codependency. I went to her intensive weeklong training called Post Induction Therapy, where I learned the concepts of looking at my past through a trauma timeline and identifying the woundings that happened along the way. I also learned through her work how we navigate trauma as children, the function of healthy boundary systems, and how they create safety in our personal relationships. I expanded on her work to create the concepts of the wounded impulsive response tool, the timeline blueprint concept, and the Emotional Response Scale. The term "functional adult" was originally coined by Pia Mellody and Terry Real.

Thank you to Babette Rothschild, author of *The Body Remembers: The Psychophysiology of Trauma and Trauma Treatment*, whose work helped me clearly understand brain functioning during a traumatic experience, how memory works, how trauma resonance is stored in the body, and the role of the therapist in creating a safe environment for others to explore and heal traumas.

Thank you to my friend Ross Rosenberg, author of *The Human Magnet Syndrome: The Codependent Narcissist Trap*. In his book, Ross explores the attraction of the narcissist and the codependent, and explains the origins of the deep wounding patterns that keep resurfacing in codependent behaviors until they are healed. Thank you for being a way-shower for so many, Ross.

Early in my psychotherapy study I was inspired by psychologist Carl Jung, who is often referenced as the originator of the concept of the inner child in his divine child archetype. Jung wrote, "In every adult there lurks a child—an eternal child, something that is always becoming, is never completed and calls for unceasing care, attention and education. That is the part of the human personality which wants to develop and become whole."[1]

Thank you to Dr. Eric Berne, author of *Games People Play: The Psychology of Human Relationships,* who developed the concept of transactional analysis. Dr. Berne also developed the idea of the child ego state, which eventually became known as the concept of the inner child. His theory describes that the ego state, or the inner child, is the part of us that holds our blocked emotional energy. In order to heal, we need to reconnect with the inner child to give that part a voice so it can release this pain. His work, along with other influencers, helped me develop more fully the idea of the responsible adult self and the age of wounding concepts.

Other thought leaders who have influenced my work are Louise Hay, author of *You Can Heal Your Life;* Alice Miller, author of *The Drama of the Gifted Child: The Search for the True Self;* Dr. Bessel van der Kolk, author of *The Body Keeps the Score: Brain, Mind, and Body in the Healing of Trauma;* and Dr. Joe Dispenza, author of *Becoming Supernatural: How Common People Are Doing the Uncommon.*

A special acknowledgment goes to my editor, Jessica Vineyard, at Red Letter Editing. Jessica, you were certainly the sherpa who guided me every step of the way, helping my dream become a reality. Thank you from my heart. Through your expert guidance and inspiration, my ideas and concepts have become manifest.

Thank you to Martha Bullen at Bullen Publishing Services for your expert guidance in helping to fine-tune the messaging of the book and

---

1 Carl Jung, *Collected Works of C.G. Jung,* Princeton University Press, 1954.

prepare it to send out to the world. To Christy Collins at Constellation Book Services, thank you for making my book look great inside and out. Each of you were my goddesses helping to birth this book. Thank you.

Introduction

You probably picked up this book because you have a relational pattern in your life that you are tired of repeating, and you just want it to stop. Maybe you have tried to do some things to change this cycle. Maybe you have tried some band-aid approaches. Maybe you have even gone to therapy, but these same tired patterns keep showing up in your life. Nothing is working.

Have you ever asked yourself the following questions?

- Why do I keep making the same mistakes in my life?
- Why do I continue to surround myself with toxic people?
- Why does it feel like I have a hole inside of me that won't go away?
- Why do I give my power away and let others determine my identity? Why don't my feelings matter?
- Why do I push people, even good people, away? Why can't I let them in?
- Why do I verbally attack others and then promise I won't do it again?
- Why do I continue to change myself for other people's comfort?
- Why is it so hard to be loved? Am I even loveable?

- Why do I doubt and second-guess myself all of the time?
- Why do I feel so hurt and angry?
- Why do I do so much for others and nothing for myself? Why do I self-sabotage?
- Why do I feel the need to be responsible for everything and everybody, and to always be in control?
- Why do I keep dating or marrying the wrong type of person for me?
- Why do I think I am a loser and worthless?
- Why do I want to run away from my life?

At one point or another, we have all asked ourselves these types of questions. Some people try to answer them on their own or ask their family or friends for help in figuring out what is wrong. This often results in getting many unhelpful opinions from others and then feeling more confused than ever. People tend to tell us what they would do, which is like getting advice from a bumper sticker.

The answers to these questions are deep within you. In your heart there is a lost, wounded *inner child* that holds wisdom and yearns for validation and healing. This unacknowledged pain is at the root of all these questions. This wounding keeps showing up in life disguised as *impulsive reactions* and overexaggerated responses.

It takes courage to even consider looking at parts of yourself that feel hurt or are confusing. Certainly, millions of people are resigned to think that this is just how life has to be. They have no desire to do the hard work to heal themselves. Many people are content to react to life in the same way over and over, expecting different results each time. The fact that you picked up this book is an indication that you are ready to listen to your wisdom and your pain, and to hear what they have to say. You are ready to heal and change how you respond to your life.

You probably know some of your patterns well, and you certainly know your emotional hurt and pain, but you may be confused about how it got this way. You know all of the things you have tried to do, what has worked, and what was disappointing.

The HEAL process—healing and embracing an authentic life—is a practical approach to help you heal and release the dysfunctional patterns that are rooted in emotional wounds, which were themselves established a long time ago. It is a transformational process that will help you to unfold and heal the wounded parts that no longer work for you, and lead you to a new place of inner healing. The process combines many approaches and exercises to help you connect with some of the underlying reasons why you react and respond the way you do. By following this transformational process, you will begin to understand and acknowledge the specific wounding patterns you are holding on to. Once you go through the process, your woundings will begin to feel more integrated with your *responsible adult self* and not feel as unknown or lost. You will not only understand why you are making these impulsive decisions, but also understand the bigger patterns in your life that are holding you back from feeling fulfilled. You will go from just emotionally surviving to emotionally thriving.

The process is not only about reclaiming the *grounded*, authentic self but also about how to recognize your *resilience* in navigating present-day difficult situations. This work will help you honor those parts of you that have worked hard to keep you safe, and to look at those parts that work against you and hold you back from claiming an authentic life. You will learn to identify the illusions and the negative, limiting beliefs about yourself that you carry. What may be unclear now as to how these impulsive reactions relate to your childhood wounding will soon become clear as you go through the HEAL process. The process will guide you to feel more whole and in control of your life.

Through the HEAL process, you will help the younger wounded parts of you, your wounded inner child that feels lost and searching, to integrate with your adult self. Until this healing occurs, the wounded part will keep being triggered, frantically stepping in front of you to take charge, and impulsively making bad decisions that your responsible adult self then has to clean up. The work you will do will help your adult self develop the tools needed to reach back through time and reassuringly take the hand of the younger wounded parts. Your adult self, feeling confident, safe, and in control, will reinforce your love for your younger self that feels lost, set strong boundaries, and tell the wounded part that it is going to be OK. You will learn to recognize how and when this younger part shows up and to ask this part what it needs to heal and integrate with the adult self. After all, we have to know where we came from to know where we are going.

Through reading real-life stories and working through the exercises in each chapter, you will see all of the relational patterns that were established in your early life. Once you see the patterns and themes that keep happening in your life, you will no longer be able to unconsciously repeat them. The moment you see the patterns—when the lightbulb goes on and everything clicks—is a moment of healing, a moment of grace. In fact, you will have many *aha!* moments as you work through the HEAL process.

Over time, you will begin to see and feel the difference in yourself as you become a conscious creator of your world instead of impulsively reacting to it. You will no longer be in the illusion of the daydream; you will be living your life present and available to yourself first, then others. Know that you will be able to transform the emotional pain that you carry, and that you can let go of the falsehood that you are destined to be burdened with emotional wounding your entire life.

Inner child work helps us get to the root of the problem—the core wounding—instead of putting a Band-Aid over the pain and hoping it gets better. I did not invent the concept of inner child work; many thought leaders who developed different ways to look at the wounded inner child came before me. I say with respect and humility that my work and inspiration are born from the efforts of many others. What I offer here is my approach to inner child work and a way to connect to your authentic and resilient self through the doorway of your wounded parts.

In my psychotherapy practice I look for how a person is functional, strong, and coping well, not just focus on their struggles or what is wrong. I look beyond their presenting pain and talk to the part that is wise, authentic, and grounded, encouraging that part to come forward. This positive psychology invites the healed part to be a champion for the wounded part. You will see as you work through this book how your wise, authentic, and resilient parts have been there the entire time, waiting in the wings for you to call on them to help your wounded parts heal.

You will find that some of the information will speak directly to your experience and some will give you a window into someone else's struggle. Even if you feel that you have too much emotional baggage to deal with, trust in yourself as you follow this process. You will begin to clearly see when, where, and how you arrived where you are today and the next steps you need to make.

As you read through the chapters, you will be looking at parts of yourself that are difficult to examine, which is completely natural and normal. You will want to have a notebook handy for the exercises in each chapter. If doing the exercises ever gets to be overwhelming, you may want to talk with a skilled therapist who is familiar with inner child work.

You can access the companion workbook for additional material, shared stories, and in-depth exercises at my website: www.theartof-practicalwisdom.com. For further reading, please see the Resources page at the back of the book. There I have listed several websites and authors from whom I have gained wisdom over the years.

Please note that definitions for italicized words can be found in the glossary at the back of the book.

The information herein is not a substitute for talking with a psychotherapist; rather, it is the approach I know and have developed from having successfully taken many people through it over the years. I have also used the HEAL process myself to heal and integrate my childhood wounding with my adult self.

Take your time and enjoy the journey. You will have a much clearer idea of yourself and how you relate to others when you come out the other side. The HEAL process is about expanding your awareness of yourself, not changing you.

Are you ready to reclaim the freedom of being your authentic self? If so, I ask that you trust me and trust yourself through this process. You are stronger than you think.

CHAPTER 1

The Walking Wounded

Late, by myself, in the boat of myself, no light and no land anywhere,
cloud cover thick. I try to stay just above the surface,
yet I'm already under and living within the ocean.

—RUMI

Have you ever noticed how some people seem like they have it all together and are good at just being themselves, and others are fragmented and scattered and have the same dramas in their life over and over?

Maybe you are one of those folks who don't understand why you keep attracting people who don't treat you very well. Or perhaps you attract people who say they are your friends but who just bring more drama into your life. What is most likely happening is that the wounded part of you is unconsciously choosing other hurt people with whom to be in relationship. Hurt people find other hurt people.

This wounding comes about innocently enough through our growing-up experiences, when we were ignored, rejected, or dismissed. For some, it comes about in dramatic ways through abuse, neglect, or other traumas. Along the way, we were doing the best we could with the tools we had at the time. However we take on this wounding, it settles deep within us, taking up emotional space and impacting how we feel about ourselves in relationship to the rest of the world.

Not everyone is affected by a traumatic event or experience in the same way. For some people a hurtful experience rolls off the back, but for others the hurt goes deep into the core. We each have our own resilience in how we process, cope, and survive beyond emotional wounding and trauma, and sometimes the trauma or wounding stays with us, tucked away as we go about our lives. We push this wounding down deep inside as we try to ignore it, because it is so painful to remember and feel again.

When we don't acknowledge the pain and the wounding, they start to come out in distorted ways, attempting to be acknowledged so we will deal with them. *Emotions* are internal messengers trying to get our attention. Most people just push the signals down or ignore them altogether.

You may have gotten used to feeling the wounding you carry and have become a member of the Walking Wounded. You may think, *I know this happened to me, but that was a long time ago, and I don't want to remember it anymore.* But the pain is going to stay with you, trying to find a way to get you to acknowledge it. It is not going anywhere until you deal with it. It is going to keep showing up, usually indirectly, throwing you off course, off balance, and contributing to depression and anxiety.

I have seen people with all sorts of wounded and traumatic histories. Many had deeply hurtful things done to them, including mental, physical, and sexual trauma wounding, often by close family members. This kind of traumatic event is often extremely difficult to think about, much less explore deeply. Most people try their hardest to forget or push away such trauma. I am often the only person they ever tell about what happened to them. The emotions surrounding these experiences need special handling and care.

If you suffered such a trauma as a child, here are some things to know:

- Nothing you did as a child warranted those things being done to you.
- The person who was doing those things was older, more powerful, and had an influence over you.
- Those things are not happening to you now.
- You are not alone. You can receive professional help to deal with this pain. You *can* heal and get past the pain.

If you feel damaged and broken from what you experienced, know there is a part of you that is intact and whole. It is the part of you that they didn't get to, your authentic part. It is the part of you that holds the key to your healing.

If I don't invest in me, no one else will.

When I was a young adult I would unconsciously pick narcissistic, wounded people as friends. I didn't know it at the time, but I eventually learned that this was a result of my wounded little boy part that instinctively knew how to interact with someone who needed attention and validation, and for me to promote them and put myself down at the same time. I didn't have to think of what to do or how to interact with this type of person because I already understood them—but I barely knew myself.

I came from an alcoholic household. The early childhood wounding caused by my home environment helped me to develop my *codependent* skill set, the tools I used to monitor and adapt myself to others who I thought needed me to do for them rather than just me being myself for them. In my healing journey I learned how to hold that pain, examine it, and work through some complicated *feelings* so that I could rejoin with my authentic self. I learned that I could just be myself and that I did not have to do anything for anyone else to have value. Using the HEAL process (healing and embracing an authentic life), I was able to heal that wounding so that I could integrate all of my fragmented parts and become a whole adult, surrounded by people who respect and love me. I now do the same for those whom I see professionally.

I often use my own story as a way to help those I am working with know they are not alone. As I tell my story, my patients hear the pain I went through and the process of self-awareness I came upon through my own therapy work. I often receive thanks after telling my story, because my experience helps the person know that someone else went through something similar and that they are not alone. Witnessing another's work is a great healing tool. We don't feel alone, we feel connected, and we grow. (You will read more of my story in chapter 3.)

> *Our pain is looking for acknowledgement.*
> *Once we connect to our wounding,*
> *a doorway for healing opens.*

I believe most people walk around with a mild form of post-traumatic stress disorder, or PTSD. I don't mean to diminish a full PTSD diagnosis or those who suffer from it, but rather to put into context that we have all experienced events that we can't shake off or that we keep replaying in our heads.

Your emotional pain is relative to you, meaning that it is most relevant only to you. Someone else may look at your story and say, "Oh, that's nothing. I had it a lot worse." Maybe they did, but this is not some sort of contest for the winner of the "Most Dramatic Childhood Trauma" award. We all carry harmful wounding, and this is your opportunity to honor and validate your feelings and finally heal.

Recycled Pain

We all carry what I call *recycled pain*, the wounding that keeps showing up when something *triggers* an old hurt. You have deeply buried this familiar part of yourself hoping to just forget it, even as you feel like you can't escape it at times.

The following is an example of a series of events that illustrates this recycled pain. This is how these wounded illusions become a part of you and how you become numb to them.

> An event happens in childhood that startles or confuses you. It is a new experience, and you don't know what to make of it. You only know you don't like the experience and the resulting feeling.

> An emotional part of you feels hurt and in pain. It stores the experience as something that doesn't feel good, or in severe cases, as a trauma. This is the initial *core wounding*.

> The core wounding, the emotional pain, gets frozen in time and at the age you were when the significant emotional event happened. (Let's say age five for this example.)

> When you get older, the younger hurt part that is frozen and is not maturing with the rest of you gets *triggered* by events similar

to the one that happened when you were five. This part reacts as though the original bad experience is happening all over again. The pain is *recycling*.

This part of you goes into action and either gets defensive and protective or shuts down, becoming quiet and invisible.

You have now developed a *wounded emotional response tool* to these specific situations. When they arise again, you automatically employ this *impulsive reaction*, your tool, to the trigger.

Your wounded five-year-old is always standing by, feeling lost and hypervigilant that something bad may happen again.

As an adult, your five-year-old that carries this *wounded emotional response tool* steps in front of your *responsible adult self* when triggered. This part makes decisions and reacts emotionally as a five-year-old would, using a five-year-old child's logic, words, and expressions. This is the origin of the expression, "You're acting like a child!"

Your responsible adult self, transfixed by this wounded illusion, is in the background watching everything, feeling helpless as the situation unfolds. The five-year-old self is strongly committed to protecting all parts of you and doesn't want the bad thing to happen again.

After the drama unfolds and completes, your wounded five-year-old goes dormant and vigilant again, waiting for the trigger to reappear.

Your responsible adult self is dazed and confused; what just happened? Why did I do that?

You begin the process of either cleaning up or ignoring what just happened, and try to move on, oblivious to the toxic recycled pain that plays out every time this wounded part gets triggered.

Dealing with this recycled pain is exhausting. Think about how many times you reenact this wounded child drama; perhaps it is multiple times each day. If this recycled pain is not healed, it will keep getting triggered, showing up, and repeating. I believe that this is a way the subconscious is trying to heal the wounding. The body, mind, and spirit are not meant to hold on to this heavy emotional weight.

How often are you in these cycles of pain? What examples are coming up in your mind regarding how this recycled pain shows up in your life? These are reactions that feel out of control or exaggerated.

Repeating Poor Choices

Another way this wounding recycles is through repeating poor choices. You probably know friends or family members who keep dating or even marrying the same type of person over and over, someone who isn't a great match for them or is not a good person. You are puzzled why someone would consciously bring someone into their life who was just like the last person they were with. You can see this, so why can't they? Perhaps you even do this yourself.

Without consciously realizing it, we often bring people into our lives in an attempt to play out these childhood wounded dramas, and the person we bring into our life as our partner often has a type of wounding that we intimately understand from our childhood. This is the root of the pattern of marrying our mother or father. We are unconsciously trying to heal this part.

Do you keep dating or marrying the same type of person? Do you keep choosing toxic people or emotional vampires as friends? Do you have the same type of reaction to an event or experience, such as lashing out and yelling or withdrawing? If this reaction is noticeable and stands out, you might later realize that you were overreacting. You may wonder why you had such a big reaction when the event itself was not a big deal. This is your wounding coming out. It happens because something inside is triggered and sets off the deep emotional wounding-recycled pain pattern. The unresolved part of you gets triggered and then makes decisions about how to react to the situation. This wounded part is tied to the original significant emotional event, and you keep repeating poor choices based on this deeply buried emotional wounding. This wounded part is not integrated with your mature, responsible adult self; it is separated out from the other parts.

Impulsive Reactions

Martin and Laura, a married couple, came to see me. Martin was prone to having big reactions to things that make him nervous. When he was triggered, he would impulsively send texts to people saying things like, *I can't keep on doing this* and *I can't take it anymore.* Understandably, friends and family who received one of these texts would become concerned about his welfare.

Laura would step in, try to make things better, and reason with him. But Martin was caught in an emotional loop, thinking and feeling that everything he was doing was bad and was not going to get better. With his lack of perspective, he was approaching the situation emotionally, but Laura was looking at it logically. They were crossing over each other, unable to hear the other.

I created a metaphor for Laura to help her understand Martin's behavior. I explained that when Martin was emotionally acting out, he was not using the language of a mature adult but the words and reactions of a much younger part of him that was overwhelmed. He was like an upset five-year-old little boy who wants someone to hear him and see his distress. Martin's wounded inner child wanted his feelings acknowledged. He did not want Laura to try to intellectually reason with him.

Laura immediately understood. This explanation helped her to understand Martin's reactions, and she was able to be more patient. Of course, Martin is an adult man with a job, mortgage, and family. He is not a young child, but there was a part of him that was stuck at a much younger time in his emotional development. When this wounded part of him got triggered by things that were overwhelming, this part thought that what happened at that young age was happening again. It would step in front of his adult self and start impulsively reacting.

Through his healing work with his wounded little boy self, Martin now finds it harder to have these big reactions because he understands the dynamic of the wounding he carries. Laura is no longer responding to him by trying to explain away or intellectualize his experience; she is attentive to his emotions and acknowledges what he feels. Martin is learning how to relate to this wounded part and how to express his feelings in a more regulated way, and Laura is learning how to listen to him in a new way.

Those who can't embrace their shadow can't embrace their light.
It's all, or it's nothing at all.

—JEFF BROWN

Impulsive reactions are the tools we use when we react to a situation from our wounded part, when we react impulsively instead of respond maturely. They become our go-to reactions to the events we experience in life. We developed these impulsive reactions over time as children and young adults, and they became part of our collection of *wounded emotional response tools* to use as needed. We bring these impulsive reactions with us through the teenage and young adult years and into our mature adult lives. We unconsciously use these impulsive tools, unaware of how doing so reinforces our recycled pain dramas.

> *Your impulsive reaction tools all work together to support the wounded narrative of your lost inner child.*

As adults, we respond to situations based on our collective experiences from birth. We develop these responses based on behaviors that were modeled by the adults in our lives or by developing responses on our own. We carry these *emotional response tools* with us wherever we go. Some of these tools help us to create better relationships, and some we use damage or destroy relationships.

There are two types of emotional response tools, functional responses and impulsive reactions (also referred to as wounded emotional response tools), and they are all jumbled together in our *emotional response toolbox*. Sometimes using an impulsive reaction tool, such as yelling or blaming, is easier because when we are deeply upset, it is easier and quicker to grab the tool of lashing out in anger rather than maturely and responsibly talking about what is happening. At other times, finding functional response tools, such as being respectful and reasonable, is easy if we take our time. We choose this type of tool when we can take a deep breath and become grounded and clear, because we have learned that when we use a wounded impulsive reaction we don't always get a good outcome.

To recap, our mature, functional responses are those we use when we feel secure and responsible. We use our impulsive reactions, which come from a place of hurt and pain, when we are not grounded and feel the need to be defensive.

We know our impulsive reactions because we have had them for a long time, and they have served us. They may not serve us well once we are adults, but they certainly helped out when we were younger. Our impulsive reaction tools helped us navigate what life gave us. They helped us in moments when there was chaos in the house or when something bad was happening. They were our wounded adapted responses to situations that felt out of our control. We used them to gain a sense of control within ourselves, even if it was just a self-made illusion. Using these reactions helped us feel better. We felt like we were making choices instead of having someone else make choices for us or project their own wounding onto us. We did not realize that we were creating a toolbox of sophisticated emotional response tools so that we could deal with what was a confusing, overwhelming world.

These tools worked for us then, but they do not often work for us today. Still, we unconsciously carry them with us and use them in our adult relationships because they are what we know.

EXERCISE: YOUR IMPULSIVE REACTIONS

Do you know what your impulsive reactions are? In this exercise you will explore some of the wounded emotional response tools you use as an adult but were crafted in childhood.

The following is a list of common impulsive reactions that are developed in childhood and then carried into adulthood. These are the impulsive reactions we have to a trigger that brings our wounding to the foreground. In your notebook, write down the ones from the list you think you learned as a child or that you have used in your adult life. On your list, circle the ones you still use as an adult. As you read over the list, gently observe. Avoid condemning or harshly judging yourself.

Why did you create these tools?

- Shutting down or withdrawing emotionally
- Being super quiet so as not to be noticed
- Acting passive-aggressive so as not to show your anger
- Blaming
- Getting too involved in a relationship too quickly
- Oversharing intimate details about yourself too quickly
- Lying
- Feeling as if you have no *needs* (*needless*)
- Feeling as if you have no desires or dreams (*wantless*)
- Self-harming as a way to self-soothe
- Sabotaging
- Overspending money you don't have to fill up a hole inside
- Projecting or mind-reading what others think or feel about you
- Using drugs, alcohol, food, pills, weed, or other substances to escape or cope
- Pushing emotions down until they manifest as anxiety or depression
- Seeking attention
- Sneaking around
- Hiding (literally)
- Overworking
- Overcompensating
- Bullying others
- Checking out
- Playing the victim for attention
- Feeling less-than
- Feeling greater-than
- Making yourself smaller so you can feel bigger

- Getting bigger so others feel smaller
- Attacking others out of anger because of the shame you feel
- Overcompensating (pretending to have it all together but feeling like an imposter)
- Rebelling at authority or those who you think are trying to control you
- Yelling
- Feeling responsible for everything bad that happens
- Getting lost in self-loathing
- Avoiding conflict
- Saying "I'm sorry" a lot
- Giving your power away
- Making everyone else more important
- Enabling others' destructive habits and avoiding real discussions
- Trying to be a peacemaker
- Acting as a caretaker
- Being a fixer
- Getting really loud or demonstrative so others hear and see you
- Ignoring others so they don't hurt you
- Giving too much or too little
- Ignoring your gut reaction or intuition
- Doubting yourself
- Being impulsive
- Being irrational
- Being moody
- Brooding
- Throwing temper tantrums
- Being clingy
- Pushing away
- Whining

- Being sarcastic
- Escaping through pornography or masturbation
- Using sex, shopping, and other activities to avoid your feelings
- Wanting to escape
- Saying you just wish you were dead (but not wanting to die)
- Wanting to be out of pain (not necessarily by dying)
- Being greedy
- Gambling
- Feeling anxious
- Changing yourself for someone else's comfort
- Being overly controlling
- Manipulating others
- Being obsessive
- Being petty

These are just some of the wounded emotional response tools you may have developed as coping skills while dealing with chaotic, uncertain, and disrupted households when you were young. They are the impulsive reactions you may use when you later sit back and say to yourself, *Why did I do that?*

(If you feel overwhelmed by reading over the list in this exercise, take a deep breath. As you go through this process you will gain clarity as to why you do these things, and learn ways to heal this wounding.)

Look within to see what other wounded tools you use that aren't listed here. Make a note of what you find, as this insight will give you clues to help you on your healing journey. You may also want to look back over your list and begin to connect with how, when, where, and why you developed these wounded emotional responses. (Save your answers from this exercise to use again in chapter 5. The impulsive reactions you identify now will show up throughout your work within the HEAL process.)

Some of these wounded tools are connected to early childhood development (e.g., yelling, raging, shutting down), while others are expressions of a teenager or young adult (e.g., drugs, alcohol, self-harm). You may have used these wounded emotional response tools because they made you think and feel that you were grown up and in control.

The various tools you put into your toolbox are a reflection of your emotional development growing up. Some of these tools were useful to you at one point, but now they are working against you. As you progress through the HEAL process, you will be transforming these reactions that no longer work for you into functional responses that are appropriate for your life today.

How Wounding Shows Up

There are many ways that our childhood woundings can show up in our adult lives. As you found in the previous exercise, these behaviors vary widely, from using sex and gambling as avoidance techniques to yelling and being sarcastic or withdrawing and becoming invisible. For example, you may have discovered that you act out by overspending, overdrinking, using pornography to escape a feeling, or getting into arguments with others. This behavior comes from the part of you that carries the wounding; it is trying to be acknowledged. Your core wounding, your lost inner child, is indirectly asking to be healed so that all of you can move on and become fully integrated.

These types of impulsive behaviors are the aspects of your wounding that never emotionally grew up with the rest of you. They are the emotionally frozen parts of you that keep repeating the patterns. You are an adult today, with adult responsibilities and many types of relationships, but the minute you hear, see, feel, or are otherwise emotionally triggered by something in your outside world, that dormant wounding awakens, causing you to exhibit, express, and interact as a much younger version of yourself. And just like a child, you may want to throw tantrums, run away, yell at the top of your lungs, break something, or sit in a puddle and cry.

> *Our woundings are an inconvenient truth*
> *that we wish would just go away.*

Let's look at how these inner woundings become triggered. Suppose that a family member was of the opinion that you were stupid when you were little. They mentioned it repeatedly, and others said something similar. You started to feel ashamed about yourself. You hid that part of you they didn't like. You didn't talk about it, denied it, and pushed it away, even though you knew at some level that it wasn't true.

Over time you began to believe that this part of you was bad and was therefore less-than or inferior. Every time someone brought it up, you would start to feel warm, uncomfortable, embarrassed, and squirmy. You wanted to hide or become invisible. That emotional wounding was becoming conditioned to be *activated* by external triggers.

Many physical issues can be related to early woundings, too. For example, I internalized many of my early childhood wounding experiences. I took in the turmoil in my family, which then lived in my gut. As a result, I had all sorts of intestinal distress as a child. My tummy aches were caused by harboring all of the agitated feelings that were going on in the household. I absorbed the emotional chaos because I was an empathic little boy, and I didn't know what to do with the intensity around me. I held my breath and pushed it down, and this manifested as an anxious feeling in my gut that I didn't know what to do with or how to name.

I tried to tell my mom what was going on, but I was literally at a loss for words. I was using the words and understanding of a young child. How could I have explained the swirling kaleidoscope of emotions that I was absorbing and that were overwhelming me? I later learned that I was also trying to protect my mom from my feelings. I didn't want her to feel bad, so I didn't tell her that I didn't like my parents yelling. I thought that she would be disappointed in me, so I just kept on getting tummy aches, swallowing my feelings, and internalizing the intense emotional energy of the household. I was protecting her, but I was also trying to protect myself.

A Word about Parents

I want to take a moment to address feelings about parents. These feelings can be highly complex, but it is important to remember that your parents or guardians, like mine, did the best they knew how. It may be tempting to blame them, or maybe you already blame them, but I would like for you to suspend that blame and see your parents in a soft gaze of acknowledgment for their efforts.

This is not about denial but about looking at your situation objectively instead of getting lost in the ego habits of blaming, shaming, and finger-pointing. Most of us have already done enough of that, either toward others or toward ourselves. This is about a respectful regard for the human experience, knowing that we all have our struggles and triumphs and that most of us have many unresolved woundings, including our parents.

I was fortunate to come from a household where I knew and felt in my heart that my mom and dad loved me unconditionally. Out of all the love, kindness, and pride they instilled in me, their unconditional love was and is a tremendous gift. It is my greatest treasure.

> *We have to learn how to give to ourselves as adults what we didn't receive in childhood.*

I know that many people did not receive the gift of unconditional love as a child. I know that parents can be less-than-stellar examples of love, but I do believe that they all do their best. I know my parents were doing their best; I also know that I needed more at times than what they could give me. The idea of this healing process is that you know what happened in the past, but now you have an opportunity to create what your inner child needs today.

OUR WOUNDING STORIES

Perhaps you resonate with what I described about my childhood but still insist that your childhood was fine. This is normal, and in fact, when I first meet with new patients, most of them tell me they had a fairly normal childhood and that nothing major happened. They developed this coping skill to help them feel better about some of the events and experiences that did happen in their *childhood family*.

Our core wounding experiences developed over the course of our formative years, from birth to age twenty, and created lifelong dysfunctional patterns in how we look at and interact with ourselves and others. These woundings created our wounding story, the *narrative* we tell ourselves about who we are, what we are like, and what we deserve. We start to believe these half-truths and untruths about ourselves. We merge our sense of self with those things we experienced. Our unhealed core wounding is the root of the emotional patterns that keep showing up in our lives.

We think, *I was abused, neglected, hurt, and rejected, and therefore I am a bad person and not worthy of much in my life.* If we don't have strong boundaries, we give others the power to create our sense of self-worth and identity, foregoing any sense of self and essentially abandoning ourselves. We begin to carry other people's woundings, their pain, and their *projections* as ideas of who we are or should be. We push down and bury our authentic selves in the process, giving up any sense of self-worth, self-love, self-trust, and self-respect.

> *We learn to hate ourselves a hundred times more than someone else hates us.*

As we grow up, we can be tempted to wrap our good and bad memories into a Hallmark movie moment, so we normalize all the bad stuff that happened by telling ourselves that "everybody" got that kind of treatment growing up. As adults, we intellectualize these experiences to rationalize and ignore our wounding. It is our intellectual attempt to try to move on and minimize what happened to us, but that core wounding is still sitting there ready to react until we deal with it.

When people tell me about their "fairly normal" childhood with no big issues, I believe them. However, I also know they have been, say, married three times and are unhappy. What they say about their life experiences and what they tell me on the surface about their childhood don't add up. They have normalized what happened to them. They are unconscious to the fact that hurtful things happened to them as children that are now contributing to their unhappiness and failed relationships. They have been telling themselves this story so they don't feel so bad or ashamed, and they promote it to others. They are not lying; rather, they are minimizing what happened and do not understand the long-term effects of those events and the wounding they carry. They are looking at what happened in their childhood using adult rationalization.

We develop this "emotional amnesia" to some of our harsher realities because we instinctively know the deep pain that lies beneath the surface. For most of us, all it takes is some scratching at the surface to reveal the wounded pain that is waiting to be acknowledged. The internalized shame we carry gets wrapped around these wounded memories and contributes to how we feel about ourselves.

> *As we heal, our minds open up space*
> *for old memories to resurface.*

It is natural for us to want to deny our emotional wounding, but the more we push it away, the louder and more insistent it will become until it finds a way out. When it does come out, it often does so indirectly, affecting our choices, our lives, and our sense of self-worth.

As children, we take in the words, judgments, and criticisms of others, essentially taking on their projected shame. We unconsciously say to ourselves, *I love this person,* or *I respect them and want them to like me. I must not be thinking the right way about myself, so I'm going to start thinking and feeling this way about myself because that's how they see me.* This is how we start to believe we are ugly, bad, wrong, stupid, ignorant, and so on. When we accept, incorporate, and carry this projected view of ourselves it becomes real to us, and we lose our connection to our authentic self.

These ideas of ourselves don't always come from outside of us, however. We can make up stories about ourselves—how we need to be better, or do this faster, or simply by comparing ourselves to someone else. Regardless of where it originated, what began as an innocent comment someone made or an idea that we have of ourselves can turn into a wounded, distorted self-concept. We accept this false perception and incorporate it into our wounding profile and narrative. This distortion stays with us until we begin to heal and neutralize this negative self-talk.

These are just a few examples of how we pick up and develop triggers that activate old woundings. There is a way out of this maze, though, by learning the right tools to use to do this work.

If we have to chase love, it isn't love. Love meets us halfway.

—JEFF BROWN

Story: Steven, an Emotionally Abandoned Teenage Boy

Steven is a thirty-year-old blue-collar man. He wanted to stay with his girlfriend, but she kept pushing him away and did not treat him very well. He persisted, and like most people who really want something, he went out of his way to try to make the relationship work. He didn't want to give up on her or the relationship, so he kept changing and adapting himself to who she wanted him to be so she wouldn't be upset. He kept giving away his power, over-compensating and compromising himself without recognizing what he was doing.

Steven's relationship was unsteady, like a three-wheeled wagon. Sometimes the wagon is upright, carrying its cargo and moving along. But then it tips over, spilling everything it is holding and scraping bottom. Steven's desire for the relationship to work was preventing him from seeing that it was not working. He continued to compensate by denying himself and ignoring his needs. He saw only the smooth movement of his relationship wagon, which was rare, and ignored all the times the wagon dumped over and spilled everything, creating a mess that took a while to put back together.

Much of the therapy process is teaching introspection. We have a lot of information, but most of the time we are not still enough to listen to ourselves. Sometimes we know that a relationship or a situation is not good for us, but we stay in denial, hoping it will change. Steven kept distracting himself with what he wanted the relationship to be instead of what the reality was.

When I asked why he thought he kept pursuing her, what it was inside of him that wouldn't give up, he said he just wanted the relationship so much and would do whatever it took. Then he said, "She yelled at me in front of a group of people the other day, but I guess I deserved it." He was ignoring the telltale signs of the abusive nature of the relationship, of being shamed, pushed away, and treated badly.

Steven couldn't see this relationship from a healed place. His responsible adult self and his wounded self were receiving all of the incoming messages, but his emotionally wounded part interpreted that he deserved this treatment—and this part was loud. He had closed himself off to what his authentic self was feeling and instead gave power to the illusion. All he knew was that when he wasn't with her he felt depressed and uncertain, so he held on tight and stayed with her to avoid feeling lonely and abandoned.

When we first started working together, he said that nothing major had happened in his life. He then went on to say that as a young boy he had been very close to his aunt, with whom he had shared many adventures and confidences. When he was fourteen, he started wanting to do other things instead of hanging out with her. He still wanted to do things with her, but his life had rapidly expanded, as he was a freshman in high school and was noticing girls. His aunt took offense to this change for some reason and abruptly dropped him from her life. She no longer checked in on him or asked him to do things, and she ignored him at family functions. Steven was devastated. He was confused, hurt, and deeply missed his relationship with his aunt. He took the hint and didn't try to connect anymore, but the hurt stayed with him.

Steven told me that a part of him died after this rejection, and he blamed himself. When he began to date girls he was very clingy, doing whatever they wanted and not wanting to disappoint them—just as he was doing with his current girlfriend. He didn't want them to leave him like his aunt had left him. His wounded part didn't want to have that feeling again.

Steven was experiencing emotional kickback from his aunt's rejection. A part of him was frozen in time at age fourteen, when his aunt emotionally left him, and this emotional abandonment had stayed with him. He had internalized the idea that he had done something wrong to create the shift in their relationship and that he was the problem.

As an adult, Steven knew only that he had lost a significant relationship once, and he wasn't going to let it happen again. As a result, he could not let go of this toxic relationship. His fourteen-year-old wounded part was holding on, desperately trying to keep this woman with him. He couldn't be fully present in the relationship because his teenage wounded self was the one in the relationship, not the grown man.

I guided Steven to write a timeline of his life during the years from birth to age twenty that described the events and emotions he remembered. (You will write your own timeline of events in chapter 5.) He quickly saw the pattern he was following from his early years. He saw that he was trying to recreate the relationship he had with his aunt. He desperately missed the closeness, the validation, and the fun and adventure he had had with his aunt, and he was trying to make the relationship with his girlfriend work to fit his narrative instead of seeing reality for what it was. This realization allowed him to start breaking the pattern.

Steven could see that he was holding on tight to a relationship that wasn't good for him so that he could avoid feeling abandoned and alone again. He thought his only choices were to either be in a bad relationship or be lonely and rejected. Once his adult self saw the cycle he was in, he felt sad and then angry at himself. He realized how much time he had wasted by dating someone who was interested only in playing out her wounding in this dysfunctional dynamic.

He began to set boundaries by becoming clear about what was OK and not OK for his girlfriend—or anyone, for that matter—to say to him. For example, it was not OK for anyone to talk down to him, ignore him, or be mean to him. It was OK for someone to respect him, validate him, and be a consistent friend.

During our time working together, Steven's abusive girlfriend dumped him, saying he wasn't the man she thought he was or the man she needed. She continued her own cycle of crash-and-burn, projecting all of her pain onto him. Now, however, he had some boundaries in his emotional response toolbox. He used these boundaries to protect himself emotionally and to tell her how he felt hurt by her comments and actions.

Through the process, Steven's fourteen-year-old wounded self began to heal. This part integrated with his responsible adult self, who was now setting the boundaries. His teenage self wasn't freaking out over the girlfriend having left because all parts of him now understood that she was toxic for him. He later realized how much of his own power he had given away in order to get her back, and he saw how he would lose himself in the process.

At the beginning of our work together, Steven was so focused on the events that were happening in the moment that he couldn't see how his early emotional wounding was getting in the way. His fourteen-year-old self was so frantic and desperate to keep her that he sacrificed himself. Now, all parts of him know how to stand up for himself, and he is learning how to not give away precious parts of himself in relationships.

THE INNER CHILD

Our access to the true self is possible only when we no longer have to be afraid of the intense emotional world of early childhood.

—ALICE MILLER

Most of us have a part within that feels younger and more immature, reactive, and out of control. We can think of this part as our lost inner child, that part of us that carries our emotional pain. Simply put, your lost inner child carries the wounded emotions and impulsive reactions that your adult self then acts out when old issues are triggered.

Sometimes the childhood *wounded self* overshadows the other parts of the personality. This part that has learned to be protective and defensive and can be loud and abrasive. It never wants anything bad to happen ever again; it is hurt and scared and frozen in place, not growing or maturing. The wounded part lives in a state of fear rather than a state of trust, and it begins to dominate the emotional landscape. Based in fear, the wounded self lashes out at anyone who tries to help, even those who are kind. This part defensively guards the wounding, believing that others are a threat.

Because this part of the personality is often so developed and large and loud, it is useful to look at how a person was before this wounding happened and the conditions within the family. For example, by his own description Steven had a relatively good childhood until his mid-teens, so we looked at how he was before then and encouraged and gave this part a voice. He was able to connect with this strong, authentic voice within to help him form boundaries as an adult.

If you are beginning to see that your wounded part is loud and dominant inside of you, try to sit in stillness with this part. In your quiet moments, see if you can ask this part to share some wisdom with you. Your inner child may be angry, smiling, happy, sorrowful, hurt, or self-pitying. It is simply asking for a voice and to be acknowledged for the deep wounding it carries for you.

In my own personal work, I learned that I was ten years old when I experienced a key wounding event. Other events had happened before and after, but ten was the age at which my emotions became frozen and held the wounding in place. I was scared and confused, and did not understand why my parents argued. I would try to be the peacemaker and attempt to control my parents so that the chaos I experienced in the household and what I felt inside would not be so overwhelming.

I believed, as most children believe, that I was powerful, that I could be the hero and influence my parents. I believed, through a child's *magical thinking*, that if I became perfect, did things that were asked of me, and never caused my parents to be mad at me, then they would not argue and my world would feel safe. But no matter how good I was, I was unable to get my parents to be loving to each other all of the time. I couldn't change my parents or their behaviors, but the belief that I needed to be perfect stayed with me. This wounding carried through to my teenage years and into adulthood.

Things that happened to us when we were children tend to have a bigger impact on us than events that happen to us as adults. When we were children our worlds were smaller, we didn't have much power or control, and our brains were not fully developed, so we perceived many experiences as highly important. As we grew up our world expanded, and because of this larger world view, we started to think that what happened to us in childhood was not a big deal.

When we look back at our childhood from the vantage point of adult reasoning, we think we should just get over whatever happened. We minimize our childhood feelings and experiences and tell ourselves that everybody's household was "like that" at the time. While this may be true, we are also looking back from the lens of an adult. We don't want to remember the bad things that happened, but they are there, waiting to be explored. The lost inner child has recorded all of these events, and they are as emotionally real today as they were then. A throwaway comment from an adult can become a defining moment for a child's sense of self.

The HEAL process will help you directly access these *wounded parts* in a safe, gentle, and loving way so that you can start to integrate your wounded child and become a whole, emotionally healthy, mature adult.

CHAPTER 2

HEALing Emotional Wounds

If you are depressed, you are living in the past.
If you are anxious, you are living in the future.
If you are at peace, you are living in the present.

—LAO TZU

The most effective therapies involve telling stories. There is something powerful about telling your story to someone else, and writing out your story for yourself is just as healing. You are acknowledging your pain, and in the acknowledgment you are saying, *Yes, this happened, but I am here now.*

In the coming chapters you will be reading stories of people I have worked with, as well as my own story. Names and identifying information have been changed, except my own, and each person agreed that I could share their story with you. Through these stories you will see that when we experience a dramatic or emotionally significant event as a child, the resulting trauma coalesces to form a core wounding within. This wounding event gets linked with the age we were when it occurred, what I call the *age of wounding*. As a way to cope with this emotional wounding, we use immature emotional response tools to interact and deal with a confusing world based on the frozen emotion originating at the age of wounding. You will learn how to personify this part of yourself so that you can begin to relate more easily to it.

Please note that I will often use the terms *wounded parts, wounded self*, and *wounded, lost inner child* throughout the book to refer to the emotionally wounded inner child. As you work through the HEAL process, you may find your own way to address your lost inner child, either by a name you were called at that age or a nickname that feels right to you today. (To be clear, the concept of a wounded inner child doesn't mean you have *dissociative identity disorder*, formerly known as multiple personality disorder.)

> *When you give your wounded part a voice,*
> *it will rejoice because the pain will finally be heard.*

Your wounded parts have been trying to communicate with you through all of the wounded, impulsive reactions you use. It has been sending codes, red flags, and sirens, but you have probably ignored them, not knowing what they meant or what to do about them. The dysfunctional ways you interact with other people are your pain and wounding coming out, trying to communicate to you and others. Some of these wounded impulsive reactions may be more developed than a child's response, but all have their roots in a painful experience.

Take a moment right now to go deeper within yourself. Think of the hurts, traumas, pains, and heavy things you carry. See if you can be still just long enough to hear the emotion or the traumatic wounding that is trying to get your attention. This could be a memory that keeps resurfacing or a feeling that comes up when you are in a certain situation. All of these feelings are natural and a part of you.

Try to hold that emotion for a bit, then move on to the exercise below.

Take a moment to identify three feelings you have right now. They could be related to what is happening in your life today or connected to an experience you remember from when you were a child. These feelings are a reflection of what is going on inside of you; they are not good or bad, they are just feelings. What are you noticing? I invite you to become accustomed to checking in with your feelings, as they carry so much wisdom for you. (If you are having trouble finding feeling words, refer to the Feelings Chart in appendix A.)

Pain of any kind stays with us until it is addressed. It is the messenger of the wounding within, and it will keep sending messages in the form of depression, anxiety, heartache, and sometimes physical issues until we deal with them. These emotions can have a great influence on the choices we make in life. It is important to recognize them so we can make conscious, grounded choices of what to do with these pain messages.

How the HEAL Process Works

Ball up a piece of paper, and then start uncrumpling it. As you uncrumple it, you can see the paper take its original flat shape again. As you smooth it out on the table, you see that some areas look smooth and intact, and others are wrinkled and misshapen. Once you smooth out the paper as much as you can, notice the original flat areas and the wrinkled imperfections. Like the paper, we all have smooth parts and parts that are wrinkled and crumpled up. Together these parts are the sum total of who we are, neither good nor bad. This is how I would like you to begin to look at yourself, as the sum total of all of your parts.

After you experience some healing moments from this work, you will have a new smoothness to some parts of you that had been all scrunched and crumpled. A kind of magic happens as you go through the process and heal, and a new, smoother, more expanded version of yourself will become easier to access. A new confidence and wisdom will come through you, and you will not react to some things as dramatically as you have in the past. You may also notice that something or someone who didn't bother you before will now irritate you and you won't know why, or that you barely notice things that used to bother you. These are all indicators that you are moving through the expansion of yourself to a bigger field. You will begin to listen to yourself more, checking in and recognizing feelings that were probably always there, and asking yourself, *What do I want to do with this now?*

Through the process of healing and embracing an authentic life you will examine those parts of you that are already healed—your functional, integrated, responsible adult self—because you are already doing more things right than wrong. You will also examine the dysfunctional, separated parts of yourself, your wounded parts that need healing.

I use the word *healing* in a present and active sense because I believe we are always healing, expanding, and growing until we transition from the planet. We are all born healed, and then we experience life with all of its tragedies and triumphs, which in turn influences and changes our sense of self.

The HEAL process looks beyond what is wrong with you to reveal what is right with you.

The HEAL process will help you to see yourself from a different perspective and with more clarity. When you begin to tie hurtful early childhood events to some of your present-day problems and reactions, you will have *aha!* moments that will shine a bright light on dysfunctional patterns. You will see clearly how your wounded inner child shows up and makes decisions that are based on a child's emotional reasoning that carries hurt and misunderstanding. Once you consciously acknowledge that what you are doing is hurtful to yourself, continuing to do so becomes very difficult.

The HEAL process is a transformational experience designed to expand your awareness of yourself. It is a dynamic process, and you will read about the journeys that others have taken as you learn how to observe and describe your own journey. You will be guided through a process to map out significant events that happened in your life from birth to age twenty. You will examine these experiences and learn to identify which ones are *emotional standouts*. The experiences that were happy and joyful expanded you and helped you to feel grounded and authentic. The traumatic or wounding experiences contracted and restricted your authentic self from becoming full, free, and open.

By discovering the core woundings that stand out, you will more easily be able to correlate those experiences, feelings, and impulsive reactions to some of your present-day adult interactions. You will begin to connect the patterns established when you were younger to your reactions today. You will also see that there is a part of you that did grow up: the responsible adult that makes the mature decisions in your life now.

The Responsible Adult Self

The *responsible adult self* is the part of you that matured chronologically, mentally, and emotionally—the part that grew up. It is the part of you that is not stuck in the past, the part that behaves as an adult, is responsible, is grounded, pays the bills, and generally does the right thing. This is the best of you. The responsible adult self doesn't always show up, but when it does, it tries to do the right thing and keeps everything moving along.

The responsible adult self did not get stuck in a dysfunctional wounding cycle. This is the part that went on and got through school, found a job, possibly a partner, and established a life in an adult world. The wounded part shows up in your adult life when your pain is triggered, but the responsible adult can step up when needed and make reasonable decisions when you are grounded and centered.

The responsible adult is the functional self that is able to set appropriate boundaries. This is the part of you that is going to help the wounded part heal. It is the part that is going to be strong, find a boundary voice, be steady, and be a champion for all parts of you. The responsible adult self is *the* most important component to making the HEAL process work successfully.

Story: Jennifer and Her Repeating Cycles

Jennifer is a smart woman who tried hard to understand why she kept making the same mistakes in her personal relationships. She chose men who did not treat her well and were in some cases abusive. Her first husband was not verbally abusive, but he was incapable of being in a committed, monogamous relationship and had multiple affairs. Her second husband had two teenage sons and a Jekyll-and-Hyde personality. He was a nice guy around family and friends but was verbally abusive to Jennifer when they were alone. He had an affair during their relationship.

Jennifer's third long-term relationship lasted twelve years. Fred was a widower who, she realized later, was a charming narcissist, controlling and abusive. He was raising three young children on his own when they met. Throughout the relationship he was verbally abusive to Jennifer and his children. She stayed with him primarily because she was afraid to leave the children alone with Fred. She made a promise to herself to stay until the last child went off to college. She was proud of herself when she left the relationship, but he wouldn't let her go. He stalked her and placed tracking devices on her car, which terrified her when she learned of it.

When Jennifer came to see me, she was depressed and confused and tired of the roller coaster. She felt good about herself at work and tried to stay positive when she came home or met up with her girlfriends, but she still felt miserable inside. As a result of her ex-partner's narcissistic gaslighting, sometimes she felt sane, and sometimes she felt crazy. She knew there was a better way, but she worried that this was how her life was going to be. Even though she had left him, she was experiencing some post-trauma symptom aftershocks from this highly dysfunctional relationship.

Jennifer began to work through the transformational HEAL process. When she created a timeline of her childhood from birth to age twenty, one event stood out when she was eight years old. She had sold watermelons for her grandfather at his fruit stand when she was a young girl. One day she was short twenty-five cents. Her grandfather, instead of being a rational adult and realizing that she had probably given out incorrect change, accused her of stealing the money. This experience crushed her. She felt horrible about letting her grandfather down, but she thought she had given out the correct change and kept track of the money. Jennifer trusted her grandfather— he must be right and she was wrong. After all, why would he lie to her or hurt her? This was her grandfather, who said he loved her, so of course she thought it was her fault.

At eight years old, Jennifer lacked the skills and perspective to set boundaries, and her mantra of "I'm sorry" began. She adopted a new way of interacting with the world: she learned to be the victim and take the blame for other people's inappropriate behavior. She was learning to trust others more than she trusted herself.

This experience was a defining moment in Jennifer's life and the story she began to tell to herself. Her age of wounding was activated at eight years old, and so began her lifelong belief that she was stupid and needed to take the blame and apologize for other people's behaviors.

In her review of her adult life choices and patterns, Jennifer could see that all three men she had had relationships with had a great deal in common. They were all narcissistically wounded, selfish, abusive in their own ways, and were never who they said they were. She discovered that all three had characteristics similar to her grandfather: they all convinced her to believe she was worthless and unintelligent, and they perpetuated her deep-seated insecurities.

As she worked through the HEAL process, Jennifer clearly saw these patterns and learned the need for healthy boundaries, both with herself and in her relationships. She saw that she sought out these particular men, and that they were attracted to her, because of her victim wounding and her idea of herself. Her wounding was trying to heal, but not in a healthy way, by unconsciously attracting these men.

She learned how to set *internal boundaries* to stop the self-talk that she was bad and wrong all the time. She learned how to stop saying she was sorry for other people's behaviors.

She developed new functional response tools to better respond to *triggering events*. She later said that the most important thing she learned was to take responsibility for herself—that she was the only one who could fix her problems—and to stop blaming the men for the way her relationships ended.

Through her self-examination, Jennifer realized that it was her wounded inner child who was staying with these men, despite her adult self knowing that she was in unhealthy relationships and deserved better. The functional response tools and boundaries she developed for herself and others provided a foundation for her to say no to future bad relationships and break the cycle.

Jennifer had spent forty-five minutes during our first appointment telling me how mean all these men had been. I said I could help her if she could work hard to look at herself and her choices, to take responsibility for herself, and not try to figure out these narcissistically wounded men. I said that we could talk over and over about why these men did what they did to her, but we would never come to a conclusion. The healing she was looking for wasn't about figuring those men out, it was about healing herself. This realization helped her redirect her focus away from others and toward the harder job of looking within.

Jennifer later told me that it wasn't always easy to face herself, but once she did, everything began to change for her. She said that healing her wounding has allowed her to love and forgive herself, and she has attracted many wonderful people into her life whom she would not have had in her circle before, and for that she feels grateful.

Functional Response Tools

You learned through Jennifer's story how she had developed a pattern of taking on the responsibility for other people's behaviors and apologizing for everything as a way to interact and control her relationships. From her early wounding, she developed impulsive reactions such as being defensive, being overly apologetic, and blaming herself. She could have stayed in the cycle of blaming these men, including her grandfather, but the blame game would have just kept her as the victim. She learned to develop the functional response tools of taking responsibility for her life choices, not blaming others and herself, and learning how to set clear boundaries with herself and others. Her responsible adult self already had many functional response tools, and working through the HEAL process helped her see how to use them not just at work but also in her relationships.

We often have good boundaries at work, as Jennifer did, but think we don't need them in our personal lives. Then we wonder why our lives are so disorganized and chaotic. We have the boundary tools, but we use them casually and not all the time. We also have a mix of impulsive reactions and functional response tools, but the skill is learning the right tool to use for the situation.

The responses in your *functional toolbox* are filled with thoughts, feelings, and behaviors that are helpful in a positive and affirming way. These tools help you to have a grounded relationship to yourself and others. They did not grow out of a place of wounding; they developed from a healed or whole place within you, and are rooted in your authentic core. You use these tools when you are balanced, non-reactive, and neutral, whether you are alone or with others. You use them when you have a clear sense of what is good for you and what is not, and when you set good boundaries. You use your functional response tools when you feel authentic, confident, self-assured, clear-headed, strong, and balanced.

When you are not grounded or clear, accessing your functional response tools may be harder because we tend to grab the most accessible tools available in a situation. If you feel fearful or overwhelmed, the easiest tool to use won't always the most functional, especially if you are off-center and feeling hurt. Shutting down or hurling insults is often easier than staying grounded, clearly expressing your feelings, and establishing healthy boundaries.

As you will read in chapter 3, many of the mature, functional tools I developed came from watching my parents and other adults when they were grounded and had clear thoughts and intentions. I learned how to be compassionate and kind, and how to extend a loving hand to help those less fortunate. I also learned functional tools by watching my grounded and authentically aligned friends to see how they handled situations.

Your functional tools and your impulsive reactions are in the same toolbox. As you work through the HEAL exercises, you will develop compassion for the wounded part of you that uses impulsive reaction tools. You will see how these impulsive tools served you at one time and how they now hold you back from having an integrated adult life.

Your functional response tools developed over time, just like your wounded tools did. These thoughts, feelings, and behaviors helped you when you were a child and may still be helping you today. They are the attributes and responses that help you stay grounded and connected to your authentic self.

The following list provides examples of functional response tools:

 Feeling proud of yourself even when you aren't acknowledged by someone else

- Recognizing the healthy and positive actions and choices you need to help you through your day
- Acknowledging the friends who are good for you and encourage you
- Honoring yourself when you have accomplished something that was really challenging to do
- Respecting yourself and your decisions
- Recognizing when relationships are reciprocal and when they are not
- Knowing that you make the best choices possible each day, even if they are not perfect
- Encouraging yourself to move forward and finding the motivation to do things that you know are right for you
- Loving those parts of yourself that still need care so they will heal
- Asking for help from others
- Practicing good self-care by getting extra rest when you need to, or participating in hobbies or sports as a way to relax
- Being emotionally vulnerable with others whom you trust
- Connecting with family and friends who help you feel whole
- Discerning who or what is working for you, and who or what is working against you

Once you have a healed perspective, your functional tools will stand out to you because you will see the positive, healthy results you get from using them. It will then become easier to access these tools instead of wounded tools.

EXERCISE: YOUR CURRENT FUNCTIONAL RESPONSE TOOLS

Using this bullet list of functional response tools, think about some of the functional response tools that help you today. In your notebook, write down the tools you use and the tools you would like to develop. Which tools do you intuitively know you need to develop?

Think about the functional response tools that others in your life use that you don't. Which ones would you like to start using? Write them down, too. (Save these notes for the exercise called "Developing Your New Tools" in chapter 7.)

GOALS OF THE HEAL PROCESS

We each have experiences that encourage and nurture our healing. The goal of the HEAL process is to encourage all parts of you to heal on an ongoing basis and reach a state of *integration* with your responsible adult self. This is a transformational, dynamic, ongoing process. You are developing new thought and feeling paradigms that will become part of you, helping you feel more complete and authentic.

Authenticity

Authenticity refers to the core of who we are. It is our true nature when we are grounded, balanced, and centered, the part that knows we are worthy of love, respect, and trust. Your authentic self has never abandoned you, but you may have buried it with illusions that you created, or ideas that were projected onto you, such as being unworthy.

We are not born with the idea that we are less-than.
It is something we learn.

We often carry illusions that were put on us by others. These illusions smother the authentic self, burying it under heavy blankets of deception and untruths. A goal of the HEAL process is to reveal the authentic self; to encourage this part to transcend those illusions; and to grow louder, stronger, and fuller. When you connect with your authentic self, life will be much easier because all you will have to do is be yourself and show up.

Resilience

Resilience is like a boat on the water that never sinks, even in rough seas. It is the part of us that resurfaces when we get turned around and over, the part that goes forward with the momentum of life. When we need to overcome or work through a difficult time, the resilient self combines with the authentic self to help us transcend overwhelming or repetitive situations. It is a source of strength and steadfastness deep within.

The resilient self, in conjunction with the authentic self, helps us to find motivation when we are in a state of despair. It keeps us strong and helps us to remember that we are lovable even when love rejects us. It is the part that keeps getting up in the morning trusting that something—anything—will be better than the day before.

Resilience is our ability to adapt, navigate, and bounce back from adverse and challenging life experiences. The resilient self holds the hope for the authentic self when we have lost perspective and think all is lost. A goal of HEAL is to reinforce and restore your resilient self to its full potential so that it is easy to draw on when you need it. Just like your authentic self, it is waiting to be encouraged and reclaimed.

Attunement

Attunement is what we use to determine our responses to specific situations. It describes how responsive we are to others and their needs and how we reflect this back to them. *Self-attunement is how aligned we are with our own life and our own needs.*

You are shaped by all of your childhood experiences, whether you think of them as good or bad, and these experiences become part of your narrative, your story. Throughout your life you are weaving a tapestry that is specific to you and your experiences. No one else has a tapestry like you do, and this is what makes you, and each of us, unique, important, and special. Self-attunement is woven into your tapestry. The level of self-attunement you have is connected to the degree that you have healed within. If you have a lot of unresolved issues and *resentments*, then it will be harder for you to be in attunement.

No one else in the world operates in the same way that you do, because the sum total of the experiences that are woven into your tapestry are unique to you. Others may have had similar life experiences, but no one has the exact same perception of the world that you have. You are tuned in, or attuned, to a specific way of seeing that embodies your unique signature. This sense of uniqueness is why we want to be heard when we tell our story to someone else. Our story is special to us, and we want to be acknowledged and recognized for our specialness.

Self-attunement is related to unique aspects of ourselves, including personality (nature), environment (nurture), and our own sense of resilience, or our ability to navigate an experience. Based on the experiences that are woven into our life story tapestry, some of us can go through dramatic and exciting experiences without a scrape, and others can go through similar experiences and feel overwhelmed or emotionally and mentally flooded, and then shut down.

Our level of attunement with others accounts for the friend who loves loud concerts, loud noises, and exciting things and the friend who treasures quiet moments, silence, and small gestures. Each one experiences life through their own lens of self-attunement. We all gravitate toward things and people that feel good to us and that match who we are, what we naturally enjoy and feel energetic about. We interpret our experiences through an attuned response lens, so something is either *synergistic* (joins or flows) with who we are or is in *opposition* (jagged and rocky) to our personal attunement.

> *When your self-attunement is clear and uncluttered with misperceptions, you can easily connect to your authentic self.*

For example, for a quiet and introspective child, speaking in front of the class in fourth grade can be overwhelming and even traumatic. It may create a core wounding moment that feels jagged and harsh. But when the class clown gets up to speak, they have a stage that suits them, so that same event may feel smooth and flowing. One has an experience that is incongruent with who they naturally are, and the other is aligned with the experience. Both children in this example are just who they are. The introvert has just as many valuable skills and talents as the extrovert; they simply experience the situation differently.

If we take this example a bit further, we see that the introvert is often encouraged to change and become more like the extrovert. But this goes against the introverted child's natural attunement. Another example is when you are not attuned to others and they are not attuned to you. These people will often try to change you because they don't appreciate how special and unique you are. They tell you what *they* are attuned to, what *they* resonate to, and everything *they* like, which, in their opinion, is better than what you like. When this happens, you are not in synergy with them, you are in opposition. This creates an opportunistic moment for confusion and emotional wounding if you don't have strong boundaries.

Wounding moments happen when others project their own perceptions onto us and we take those projections to heart. When you were young, for example, a parent or friend might have asked, "Are you going to wear *that*?", or your parents might have asked you why you wanted to play volleyball or disapprovingly questioned why you were interested in a subject like ornithology. Such scenarios sound innocent enough, but when we hear these comments over and over, the messages go in. This is where negative self-talk, such as *I'm a bad person, I'm so stupid, Why can't I do this better? Why are they mean to me?* and *What did I do wrong?* comes from. We began to replay other people's words in our heads and started believing them.

This can create a lifetime habit of thought and feeling, of doubting oneself, questioning things, and being fearful of what others may say. People who struggle with such self-doubt are still attuned with themselves, but they have lost the connection to their sense of who they really are, their authenticity. They close down to their authentic self because they have given so much power to other people. They have come to believe this cloudy and incorrect perception of themselves. There is dissonance between the illusion of themselves they adopted along the way and their authentic self.

Those who have a clear connection with their attunement and authentic self don't care what others say about them. They have strong boundaries and can shrug it off and not take it in. They are clear with their attuned response—their authentic sense of self—and their resilience and synergy are strong. Because of their consistently strong internal boundaries, they are able to stay aligned to their authentic self.

In summary, cultivating and maintaining a clear self-attunement—how you experience and interpret all of the interactions in your daily life—is a goal of the HEAL process.

Discernment

When you were young, you used *discernment* when you clearly didn't like something or didn't want to do something. Your discernment, or what you thought about that thing, was clear and focused. Over time, other people and events influenced you and may have interfered with your ability to discern what you liked and what you didn't like, and your sense of self became blurry. From a place of loving and trusting others, you began to give them power to determine your sense of self-worth and identity.

Discernment is the decision point between doing something mindfully and reacting impulsively. Learning to discern the difference between your sense of self and someone else's idea of you is an important part of the HEAL process.

The exercises you will do throughout the chapters will help you to learn the art of personal discernment. A goal of the process is for you to know, at a deep gut level, those with whom you are synergistically aligned and those with whom you are not. Learning to have clarity in your discernment is key to keeping strongly aligned with your authentic self.

The HEAL process will also help you to discern how you truly feel about yourself. You will learn whether your idea of self came from someone else or from your interpretation of life events. The art of discernment will help you to develop the ability to stand back and see that you were not born with the idea that you are bad or less-than, and to determine where that idea came from.

EXERCISE: SELF-DISCERNMENT

Take a few moments to determine your skill at self-discernment with the following questions. If you need more prompts, you can refer to the self-reflection questions in the introduction. In your notebook, answer the following questions that apply to you:

- What is jamming your authentic, clear perception of self?
- How do you sabotage your life?
- What negative beliefs do you have about yourself? Where did they come from?
- Why is it hard some days to know you are loved?
- What sort of situation or person feels good to you? Why?
- What sort of situation or person does not feel good to you? Why?
- Why do you let others influence your choices most of the time?
- Whose voice is inside your head?
- Why do you think you doubt a choice or decision you made and then backtrack?
- How often do you make choices without even thinking about them?
- In what situations are you mindful of your choices? Why these situations and not others?
- With whom in your life do you have a difficult time knowing where they end and you begin?
- What feeling or idea do you carry that you adopted from someone else?
- From whom, where, or how did you acquire the belief that you are less-than?

Look over your answers. What themes do you see? Are there situations or names that you listed more than twice? What is the message you are discovering about your level of discernment?

If you responded to only a few of these questions, you may have a strong connection with yourself, know yourself very well, and make good choices. If you filled a page or two with responses, and wrote down many of the same people and situations, then you need to work on gaining clarity by using your discernment. If you have a lot of drama and dysfunction in your life, you probably need to do more work in your ability to discern situations and other people.

You have the ability to be discerning; you just learned to give away your power to others so they would like or love you. You made their needs more important than your own because of poor boundary setting.

Discernment is about clarity within ourselves, not confusion. If you are confused about why, when, and how you think or feel about something, then keep reading. Each step of the HEAL process will help you to develop a clear idea and connection to who you really are.

Unfreezing the Wounding

As you have read, some of the goals of healing and embracing an authentic life are to develop and honor your authenticity, resilience, self-attunement, and discernment. While these are important goals in your healing, they serve to support a deeper goal: to heal the younger, emotionally wounded part of you that is frozen in time so that it can integrate with your responsible adult self and allow you to become emotionally free. Healing this frozen part so that it does not continue to show up and make bad decisions is vital to your overall healing.

As you learned in chapter 1, this part of you is a wounded slice of your emotional development that is stuck and frozen in time. It is the part that is always on the lookout for a situation that feels like the original wounding event. The resulting wounded response pattern keeps repeating until you recognize and then heal it. Once it is healed, the part that holds the memory no longer becomes triggered, and you will no longer repeat the same patterns over and over. In other words, you will have a clear connection with your authentic self.

Boundaries

Boundaries help us to have a sense of safety in our personal relationships. In chapter 4 you will be learning how the lack of boundaries keeps your wounding stuck, and in chapter 6, you will learn how to create functional boundaries. For now, know that boundaries are your gut reaction to a situation. Boundaries come from the part of you that knows immediately whether you like something or not.

When we have strong connections to our boundaries, we know that we can look out for ourselves. *Internal boundaries* are commitments and agreements with ourselves about what is acceptable or unacceptable. *External boundaries* are statements or actions that we make to others that establish what we want or don't want. In the context of the wounded inner child, the younger self needs to know that the responsible adult self is going to be there for protection and to set strong functional boundaries so the inner child does not get lost and hurt again. The wounded part looks to see if the responsible adult self is going to set boundaries in dysfunctional or chaotic situations.

There are many ways that people develop a homegrown boundary system. Most people have some boundaries that they use, and if they had good boundary role models in their childhood family, they are probably doing a good job of establishing boundaries in their adult relationships. But those who did not have good boundary role models often have inconsistent, broken, or nonexistent boundaries. When good internal and external boundary systems are lacking, a feeling of safety in personal relationships is missing.

Many people did not have a strong boundary system when they were children, and didn't know that they could even set boundaries. The wounded part was all about self-protection, using wounded tools to try to defend instead of using appropriate boundaries to protect. This wounded part will keep stepping in front of the adult self using impulsive reactions until the responsible adult self sets clear boundaries.

Boundaries are a way for us to create a sense of personal, physical, intimate, emotional, and mental safety with someone else. Being able to set good boundaries allows us to maintain our sense of self when we are in a challenging or threatening situation. Having boundaries means saying no when we mean no. It means having a clear connection to our authentic self so we know how we feel about something.

Children who grow up in dysfunctional environments do not learn how to set good boundaries, and the boundaries that are in the household are typically not enforced. I learned to always put others first and to make others' needs more important than my own. I kept shoving my emotions down, and the intensity I felt inside had to get really bad for me to finally say my big no. Even when I did say no or yell or become angry, I did not know how to maintain good boundaries. My boundaries were not clearly defined in my family, and I never really knew what situations I was responsible for and what my mom and dad should own. Because of this ambiguity, or *enmeshment*, I ended up with the idea that I should be the one to carry the blame when things were chaotic in the household.

Functional boundary systems are the glue that makes the HEAL process work together. You will learn the steps to take to establish good boundaries so your wounded parts know that they don't have to be on the lookout all the time. You will learn that you don't have to carry someone else's wounding, and you will learn where you end and they begin. Once you learn to set boundaries, you can not only survive negative encounters but thrive in your life.

Integration

The final and most crucial goal of healing and embracing an authentic life is to create a foundation of support and encouragement for all of the wounded parts to *integrate* with your responsible adult self. Through your introspective work, this integration will bring together those parts of you that are stranded, frozen in time, and stuck.

Through your work to encourage your responsible adult self to step forward and set strong internal and external boundaries, your wounding will feel much less raw and unhealed. Your expanded awareness will allow you to see the impulsive and destructive patterns, giving you the power to change your responses to situations. As you heal, this wounded part of you will no longer be triggered, and it will have softer edges. You will still have your memories of what happened, but they won't have as much charged emotional energy around them.

As the wounded part heals, it will no longer be isolated, dormant, and waiting for the next trigger. It will mature emotionally to integrate with the responsible adult self.

Story: Anya, a Brave Little Girl

Anya is an accomplished, professional thirty-two-year-old woman. Her parents are first-generation Americans. As teenagers, her parents emigrated separately to the United States, where they met, fell in love, went to work, and had two girls, Anya and her sister, Kiara. From the outside the family looked like it was living the American dream, but there was no happiness inside the house. Anya's mom and dad worked opposite shifts, so the two children were shuttled between older relatives in their building and neighbors whom they didn't know well.

At nine years old, Anya's mother told her that she was to be the adult in the house until their dad got home. She was now responsible for six-year-old Kiara, so Anya became "little Mommy." Her mother also told her that she had to make sure her father didn't drink when he came home, as her mother worked second shift and their dad worked first. Anya had to get dinner on the table, make sure Kiara got her homework done, and hide the liquor bottles or distract her father long enough to keep him from drinking too much so that when her mom came home, she wouldn't be mad at Anya for how drunk their father was. Whew! That is a lot for a little kid.

It was clear from her story that Anya suffered many core woundings. The more we talked, and the more she worked on her childhood timeline, the more she remembered. The therapy process gave her nine-year-old self a safe place to vent her feelings about all of the situations and feelings that no one in her family could hear. She began to connect with the feelings of her younger wounded self, and saw how those same feelings were still coming out in her adult life. She said it was like she was pulling back a big curtain and clearly seeing for the first time the emotional struggle she had suffered in her early life.

Anya began to see how much pressure her mother had put on her at such a young age. At the time, she was made to feel that this level of responsibility wasn't strange or unusual, and her parents didn't let her complain or have any feelings about it because they needed her to "pull her weight" to make the family work. Anya's parents were relying on a child to do an adult's job, so Anya's childlike ways of playing, dreaming, and having a sense of freedom had to be put aside for survival. She could no longer be just a kid; she had a schedule and duties beyond her capabilities, and she had to manage and be responsible for her father's alcoholism. She was becoming, in codependent terms, the *caretaker, fixer,* and *controller,* and becoming *needless, wantless,* and highly focused on other people. Unfortunately, no matter how hard she worked, it wasn't enough. She wasn't able to make anything better, and she was swimming upstream all the time.

Her parents did not acknowledge any of Anya's struggle, which created anger and resentment in her that built up over the years. Now, as an adult and married with children, Anya didn't know what to do with these feelings of frustration from a situation that she couldn't go back in time and fix. Even in adulthood, Anya saw her mother continuing to put her in the role of taking care of everyone else. Her mother projected onto her that she should feel guilty if she did anything for herself. Anya loved her parents and was still trying to help them, but she felt overwhelmed and hopeless, and thought that the cycle would never end.

She eventually realized that a key emotional standout from her childhood was feeling unappreciated. Her little-girl feelings could have been validated if her parents had recognized and appreciated the weight of the responsibility she took on as a young child, but they were caught up in their own lives and were unaware of how impossible it was for a little girl to take on adult responsibilities.

As part of her HEAL process, Anya wrote *healing letters* back and forth to her younger self. She said this exercise gave her a great a sense of relief, as she was finally acknowledging and validating all of her hard work. She cried a lot for her little girl, as she was at last giving herself permission to look at the absurdity and enormity of what she had been asked to do as a child and the emotional burden that she carried. She had to grow up really fast, develop her cognitive skills to be strategic in planning and execution, and had no time or place for her feelings.

In cases like Anya's, feelings are often pushed deep down inside. Children in such environments learn that their feelings aren't going to help them, that they will only make things worse. These children grow up to be highly analytical and logical, almost unfeeling, because they had to use all of their brain power to literally think their way through complicated situations in order to survive emotionally.

People who are highly analytical and overly reliant on their intelligence and push down their emotions probably learned at a young age that doing so was better than feeling their feelings.

Today Anya works at an extremely analytical job. She can read people well and knows whether someone is having a good day or a bad day. She also knows how to adapt herself to accommodate someone else's mood. These are all wounded emotional response tools from her childhood that she carried with her into adulthood. These skills do help her in some ways, but her willingness to be a caretaker can be distracting, as she often attends to others instead of taking care of her own needs.

Anya finds it important that things be in order and under control, with absolutely no surprises. After all, she learned at a young age that she had to have control in the house or her mother would be mad at her. As she got older, she developed animosity toward her mother because of the unrealistic expectations that were placed on her. She often took out this anger on her husband.

Through her work to understand herself, Anya's responsible adult self began to recognize when her younger wounded and hurt parts became triggered and impulsively tried to control and "survive" everything. Her responsible adult self was sad that these impulsive reactions were a result of all the pain and emotional struggle she went through as a child. As a result, much of her healing was centered around kindness and compassion for all the hard work her wounded little girl self had to do to make her complicated household as functional as it could be.

As Anya worked on her timeline, her letters to herself, and her self-awareness, her relationships with her husband and mother softened. She was able to get out of the survival/control mode she had been using for decades, and was able to relax and enjoy her life more. She also learned to set boundaries with herself and with those around her.

She is recognizing that she is expanding and transforming but that her mom still behaves the same. The difference is that Anya no longer does whatever her mother asks of her. She now verbalizes how she feels when her mother talks down to her or ignores her struggles. Her little girl has found a voice, and her adult self is finding the words to use to set boundaries with her mother.

Anya's responsible adult self now reminds her wounded little girl self that the events from childhood are no longer happening. She reminds her younger self that she is safe, that she can set boundaries with those around her, that she is emotionally safer today than she has ever been before, and that she has a loving husband who helps with their children.

As you work through the HEAL process and heal your emotionally wounded inner child, you will find that those around you are not changing as you are; we can't change and control others. However, you will be transforming and expanding yourself and your relationships from the inside out.

We have to learn to give to ourselves as adults
what we did not receive in childhood.

CHAPTER 3

The Lost Inner Child

Heal the boy and the man will appear.

—TONY ROBBINS

Many people don't realize that they have a lost inner child who makes a lot of decisions in their adult life that the responsible adult self later has to clean up. They go about their lives on auto-pilot, impulsively reacting, yelling at the top of their lungs, withdrawing and sulking, or keeping others at arm's length because they are scared of emotional connection. They feel hurt, confused, abused, shamed, or neglected, just like they did as a child, but now they look and sound like an adult. They are unaware that a part of them is lost and emotionally stuck in place. Many people are scared to look within because they know at some level that something powerful is lurking in the shadows, carrying all of those feelings they want to avoid.

The lost inner child is a part of you that is emotionally frozen in time. It is "lost" in the sense that you may be oblivious to what will later be obvious signs of communication from this part. Even though this is a part of you, it is lost because it didn't mature emotionally with the rest of you.

Here I tell my story so that you can see how the inner child becomes lost, trapped, and desperate to communicate, and how it can ultimately be found and healed.

MY STORY

I was born in Louisville, Kentucky, in 1961. Growing up in the upper South in the 1960s was a wonderful time filled with long, hot summers, when I would escape into nature and come home with my pockets filled with rocks and sometimes frogs. It was the jet age, with fins on cars and rocket shapes and orbital patterns on things that had nothing to do with space exploration. It was a time of hope and optimism, but there was also a lot of racial unrest and protests. The nightly news, in black and white, would tell of the twisted carnage of the Vietnam War as I sat on the braided rug and watched in horror, confusion, and sadness. I clearly remember my dad asking me, when I was about five or six, if I would go off and fight in the war. This was an absurd question to ask a child, but with absolute certainty I said no, which, in retrospect, was the first time in my childhood that I made a conscious firm boundary statement.

I came from a large, extended family and was close to many of my relatives. I had some cousins who I rarely saw, though, so I was not always clear about which brown-haired kid was from what part of the family, much less what their names were. I learned that there was a Southern order of things, and proper manners and courtesies. There was a hierarchy of those who aspired to be well-to-do and the majority, who were just making do.

I was fortunate to grow up within a loving, intact family, with my mother at home caring for me and my younger sister. My father diligently worked hard at the same company for more than forty years, providing a comfortable lifestyle that put us solidly in the middle class. When I started high school, my mother returned to work at the company she had worked for before she married my father. Both my parents now worked for blue-chip companies, where they had a sense of place, connection, paternity, and longevity.

My parents created an environment in which I knew, in the deepest part of myself, that they loved me and would care for me. This solid foundation established a firm sense of unconditional love and resilience in me. They did their best raising my younger sister and me, even as their lives became more complex. The increasing pressure, though, led to yelling and my father's alcohol abuse, and my mother's physical illnesses created emotional ups and downs of uncertainty. My mother was the chief enabler, dancing to my dad's poorly chosen outbursts of emotions.

In this dynamic, I learned the skills of the *codependent*, a category of behaviors, or skills as I call them, used to adapt to stressful or dysfunctional situations. The codependent skills I learned during this time were the first wounded tools I put into my toolbox. These emotional response tools were immensely helpful to me early on as I tried to figure out how to emotionally navigate my family. I was also in the process of developing a *false self*, a self apart from my authentic self. I was learning how to deny my own needs and push down my feelings. Beginning at around the age of six, in order to help my mom and dad and to relieve their stress so they wouldn't argue, my little boy self thought, *I'll just do everything they ask of me perfectly, and then they won't yell and argue and my dad won't drink and rage.*

This is a classic case of the child of an alcoholic taking on responsibility for the parents' behaviors. I believed I could control my parents' situation by changing myself. I was the oldest child and took on all the qualities of the firstborn in a family where alcohol is the main igniter of high emotion. I learned to be frightened of angry people, beginning with my dad; I sought out approval from others by overcompensating, primarily from my mom; and I developed an overwhelming sense of responsibility for the entire household. I felt all of the high emotion in the house intensely. I didn't know what to do with these feelings, so I internalized them. The house was filled at times with electric tension, flashes of quick anger that manifested within me as worrisome thoughts and sadness. Then, confusingly, the polar opposite would happen, and we would experience moments of contentment and even joy.

My sister was born when I was seven. I was so used to being an only child that I was confused and hurt when she came along, but she eventually helped me not feel so alone. There were two of us now, and I became protective of her.

In my early years, from age six to eleven or so, I would become so overwhelmed that I would go to my room and cry face down on the bed. I tried hard to conceal my emotional outbursts because I thought that I shouldn't display emotion. After all, I was focused on my parents' emotions, and I didn't want them to be upset with me. I was a very confused little boy. My mom, and sometimes my dad, would come into my room, sit on the edge of my bed, and gently ask me what was wrong. I could hear and feel their sincerity and concern, but they did not know what to do to make me feel better.

Their outreach was comforting, but I wasn't able to articulate the feelings I was feeling, although I do remember saying to my mom that I wished she wouldn't argue with my dad. Their yelling frightened me to my core, and I felt that the entire house was going to explode with the intensity of their arguments—or was it the intensity of the feelings I had inside? They saw that I was in distress, but they couldn't see their part in my confusion and pain. They couldn't see the cycle of everything being fine, and then changing as my dad, feeling anxious, drank a beer with a chaser and my mom tightening her lips in anticipation of a bumpy night. There I was, right with them, holding my breath and feeling my stomach clench.

I was using a number of wounded emotional response tools in order to cope, including being a caretaker, peacemaker, enabler, and conflict avoider. I felt needless and would isolate, become emotionally withdrawn, and try to be invisible. I practiced reading others, tried to control the situation, compartmentalized my emotion, and internalized that emotion into intestinal distress. Using the wounded tools I was developing, I tried to make it all better. I tried to be the hero and rescue the family.

I learned how to separate out my emotions and compartmentalize my inner life into different selves as a way to survive the intensity. I tried to make sense out of my deeply confusing feelings. I developed the tool of compartmentalization during my early years to cope with the emotional intensity of the household. Because I was shutting down and not talking about my feelings, I would often go into states of depression and sadness. On the outside I wanted others to see that everything looked fine, but inside I felt empty, ineffectual, and lonely.

I tried to become someone I thought my parents wanted

me to be. I would watch their expressions and the way they walked, and listen to the tenor of their voices to see if it was a good day or not. I would look at their facial expressions to determine how I needed to change myself to help them out. Should I approach them and tell them about my day? Is this a good time to ask a question? Should I just be quiet and read or watch television, or should I get out of the house and go play by the creek? I was becoming an expert at reading people, and that tool went into my emotional toolbox.

Escaping into nature was a perfect way for me to self-soothe and ground back into myself. I would go down to the creek in the woods with my Matchbox cars and toy army men. I was trying my best to cope, and the isolation was restorative; it was a relief from the pressure in the household.

This withdrawal and isolation, signs of traumatic stress in a child, became two of my key coping skills. They later developed into the wounded emotional response tools of withdrawing into loneliness and not speaking my true feelings as I got older. I also developed the art of personal reflection, meditation in nature, and exploring as ways to reconnect with my authentic self. These became functional emotional response tools.

I was no different from my friends—or any other kid—in that I only knew my world. I was trying to figure out my confusing home life, and my solution was to change myself to accommodate the situation. The more I put expectations on myself that I should be able to handle the situation better, the more I began to think that something was wrong with me when this didn't work. I thought I should be able to figure out why my parents were arguing; I thought I could make it all better and control their emotions. When they argued, I was not doing my job well enough. I thought I was failing at my job, that I wasn't doing something right, that I was flawed.

I was developing a narrative about myself that I was *less-than*, or not good as others. I took on this illusion of self, and it became real. This misperception of self began to shut down my authentic self. I didn't think I could be me; I needed to do for others and not give to myself, as I wasn't worth that.

As my sister and I grew up, most days were pretty boring and mundane; my parents worked, I walked home from school, and when my sister was older, we came home together. I looked out for her, we did our homework, and in the evenings we all watched television in the family room. On the weekends my dad hitched up the boat to the car, my mom got the food and cooler ready to go, and we drove to a lake or the river, where we spent all day out with friends, having a blast. We came home like tired, soggy dogs, and fell into a deep, contented sleep.

I was a highly sensitive kid, so even with all this family normalcy, I learned to watch for things about to take a turn for the worse. I could go from feeling free and open to being hypervigilant, watching my mom and dad's every move. I never knew when it was going to happen, and the random nature of the outbursts was unnerving.

My little-boy brain and heart began short-circuiting because the good times would get cut short by yelling and chaos. I started creating a false self as I suppressed big parts of myself to adapt to the environment and my family. I was giving more power and energy to this false self, the perfect Bobby self that believed he could control and change adult behavior and emotions. I was in a state of *magical thinking*, believing I could control the household, to make it happy—or at least calm—all of the time.

My mom was also trying to make the household calm and emotionally safe in her own enabling way. I learned that it wasn't going to be a good night if we didn't prepare the house before my dad got home from work. From as early as I can remember up until I left home to go to college, I took on my mom's wounded emotional response tools as chief enabler and martyr, and the burdens that went with them. I could see and feel the tension she was feeling, so I became *enmeshed*, or entangled with her emotions. I didn't know where her emotions ended and mine began. I was a little boy who not only had the job of being a little boy but also the responsibility of taking care of my mom and managing my dad's mood so he wouldn't get mad and yell at us.

Even though my dad drank and raged, I knew he loved me. He wasn't an ogre, he wasn't a mean man, he just had emotions (primarily undiagnosed anxieties) that he didn't know how to express in a functional way. I remember, beginning around the age of eight or nine, sitting in the family room watching television, hearing the garage door open, and thinking, *OK, what am I in for tonight?* My stomach would tighten, and I would listen to the sound of his footsteps to see if they were light or heavy ones. I would watch him enter the family room and read his face to see how he was doing. *Does he look upset? Is his face scrunched up? Are his eyebrows low or high? Did I do anything wrong today? Or—wait—does he look relaxed?* My emotions were complicated because on the one hand I was glad to see him, but on the other hand I never knew which version of my dad was coming home that night.

After an outburst of anger and the foreseeable drinking subsided, my dad would try to make amends and connect. He showed me how to build things, took us on trips around the country, and gave me a much richer quality of life than many of my friends had. He sacrificed his time, money, and energy to build a multidimensional childhood for my sister and me. He was a man with his own complex emotions and inner pain, but he did not know how to express them effectively. I had to develop a set of emotional response tools similar to my mom's so that I could find my place and join with him.

Once I was an adult, my mom would tell her friends, "We never had any problems with Bobby, he always did what we asked." Well, of course Bobby did; that was Bobby's J-O-B. I took on the responsibility of doing everything right. What pressure for a little kid!

I clearly remember one incident from when I was ten years old. My mom and dad were in the kitchen arguing, and my sister and I were on the couch in the family room; she was on "her" side and I was on "my" side. We heard them arguing in the kitchen, but we kept watching television as if everything was OK, because that is what codependent children do—we pretend. Their yelling back and forth got louder than it had ever been, much louder than the television set.

I became extremely stressed and overwhelmed, and wanted to crawl inside myself or have the couch swallow me up so I could escape. As their yelling continued to escalate, I moved over next to my sister to form a buffer between her and them. I wanted to protect her from the intense emotion and shield her from the blast of anger, but it kept up. Louder, more intense, more swearing. I had to get her out of there, I had to protect my sister, so in a big wave of courage, I took her hand, led her back to her room, and slammed the door shut behind us. We silently sat on the edge of the bed, and I just held her. Neither of us said anything as my parents continued to argue. Suddenly it got quiet, and then there were footsteps.

I was terrified, as perfect little Bobby had defied the family dance. I was standing up to the wall of anger and dysfunction, and I was saying no. I had no idea what was going to happen, but I knew I had to get my sister out of the family room for her safety. I didn't think about myself. I was following the playbook typical for codependents, as we are able to set boundaries to protect another person, but we will not necessarily do the same for ourselves.

My dad, red faced, opened the door and saw me with my arms around my sister. He told us that we needed to come back out to the family room *now!* He wanted us to return to the family dance, but that was the last place I wanted to go to. In a moment of time-stopping clarity, I wasn't scared. For the first time, I really felt brave. I reached deep inside and found my authenticity, my resilience, and my determination. I said no. He reached over, grabbed my arm and my sister's, and took us back out, placing us on the couch. He wanted everything to go back to "normal."

I don't know what was going on in his mind, but I am sure that some part of him realized what he was doing with his out-of-control anger. But I was fed up, and I had found a lot of courage to try to break out of and disrupt the family cycle. I was fundamentally saying that this couldn't happen anymore. I was tired and overwhelmed by their arguing, and I didn't want my sister to experience what I had for the first ten years of my life. I didn't want her to be wounded by their dysfunctional dance. I thought, *I'm in this dysfunctional dance with you two, but you're not going to get her.* I knew that I couldn't fight or argue with my parents, but I could express my feelings with my feet and protect my sister. I remember everything from that scene—time of day, lighting, furniture, where everyone was standing or sitting—which is what makes this event one of my more emotionally traumatic memories.

(I would like to take a brief tangent here and explain what happens in the brain during and as the result of a trauma. When we have a traumatic experience, our brains record everything so that if the event were to happen again, we would know the warning signs and get ourselves to safety. This is a primitive survival response that happens deep in the brain, in the amygdala and the hippocampus.

During a traumatic event, the amygdala acts as the brain's command center, assessing what action to take next based on the incoming data. It communicates with the rest of the body through the central nervous system to give us the energy to fight, flee, or freeze. In normal situations, the hippocampus puts a time stamp—a beginning, middle, and end—on all the events in our lives. During a traumatic event, however, the hippocampus is suppressed, and the traumatic memory doesn't get stored like other memories. This is why, when we are triggered by something that reminds us of a traumatic event long after it is over, we re-experience the event through flashbacks; part of the brain doesn't know the trauma has ended. This is also why some memories come back over and over.)

As I neared adolescence, I knew I needed to protect myself from my parents' relationship, but I didn't have any functional tools. At times I would have flashes of recognition of setting a boundary and feeling empowered, but most of the time I went back to the wounded impulsive tools that I started creating when I was a little kid.

When I was in my early teens, my mom began to have surgeries for various reasons. She would instruct me on what to get out to cook and how to put it together. I always tried my best to rise to the occasion, but this was different, as I had never cooked before. Cooking became a physical demonstration of what I could do to help the family and make things better. No matter how tired I was, I did all my chores and homework, then overextended myself and gave away all of my energy for the family. This lack of self-care was reinforced by the false self I had developed, because my authentic self was so shut down and cloudy at this point.

I also was trying to figure out how to make things better with my dad, but I was resentful of his anger and behavior. I was angry myself, and resented that he couldn't control himself. It didn't make sense to me how this man who I knew loved me, who had kindness for others, and who created wonderful experiences for me and my sister would also rage and say mean things. I was going through puberty and was even more confused, emotional, overwhelmed, and exhausted by the chaotic emotional dance with him. Then one day something in me just broke.

During my teenage years I was on emotional autopilot. I had adapted to my environment, and I was growing up and maturing. But even though I was physically getting taller and older, I didn't feel older inside; I still felt like a hurt and confused little boy. I still reacted the same way when my dad got upset or my mom was sad. I had battle scars inside from all of the emotions I had absorbed, I had my playbook, and I knew what to expect. I felt emotionally beat up, I didn't have good boundaries, and I had to forgo my sense of self in order to help and be present for others. I was still working my full-time job as the hero in my dysfunctional family.

I knew as a teenager that I wanted to go into a helping profession, which was natural considering the early childhood apprenticeship training I had. During my first years of undergraduate school I worked at a private mental hospital as an orderly. This experience took my caretaker, rescuer, and fixer skills to a whole new level. Working at the hospital was my own version of immersion training into the mental health field. It was 1980, so imagine the institutional white shirt, white shoes, and white belt. It was right out of the classic movie *One Flew over the Cuckoo's Nest*.

I was assigned to work on the men's intensive care intake unit. This was where the patients who were the most severe—literally out of their minds and acting out—were first admitted. I had a unique vantage point to see severely mentally ill patients walking around in a catatonic state, drugged out of their minds, shuffling along, or staring into space.

At this time, new medications for mental health care were slowly being introduced, but for the most part there were just a small number of therapies and only a few anti-psychotic medications available to help patients with their symptoms. These broad-acting, brain-flooding drugs produced zombie-like responses in patients, but when I saw these large men out of their minds, I was grateful for the drugs. This was an era of long-term institutionalized asylum care for the "lifers," the patients who were admitted when they were young, with budding mental illness raging, and stayed for most of their lives. I took patients to receive their electric shock therapy (today known as Electroconvulsive Therapy or ECT), stayed in the room as psychiatrists administered the procedure, and then escorted them back to their rooms.

Even though I had received training and knew the safety

protocols, there wasn't much that could prepare a skinny eighteen-year-old to deal with a wild-eyed grown man, in the midst of a psychotic episode, who wants to kill you as you and the other orderlies restrain his hulking body onto a bed with leather straps. My early childhood training of compartmentalizing my emotions and stuffing down my feelings helped me to stay calm in the midst of their psychotic delusions, hallucinations, and manic episodes. Thanks to watching my dad rage and my mom compensate by not showing her emotions, I had a toolbox full of emotional response tools ready to go when I clocked in at the hospital.

My parents wondered why I wanted to work at "the crazy hospital on the hill." I couldn't explain it other than I was interested in psychology. I now realize that I felt a great empathy and connection to these emotionally wounded individuals. I wanted to study psychology to figure myself out, and I thought that I could relate to the emotional suffering of these patients. I was maturing into a grounded world of feeling my own personal power, but I also knew the wounded feeling of being hurt and overwhelmed with emotions. I could contain my own emotions, so I could sit with these patients in the middle of a psychotic break. In a way, they were my people.

After two years at a local university, I left home to go to Loyola University of Chicago. At this point everything changed for me and for my sister. I was twenty years old and free from the dysfunctional dance, but when I left, my sister moved to the front line. I was no longer the buffer between my parents and my sister. I was no longer there to read everyone's mood, moderate, smooth things over, and try to make it all better. These were skills I had developed to make the household as functional as I could. When I left with my unique wounded codependent tools, my sister was left alone with them, and she had to develop her own set of skills.

She had her own breaking point with our parents in her high school years. She would have to pull over when driving to high school from crying so hard after dealing with their arguments and stress at home. Sometimes she could not go to school because of being so upset. Our mom never questioned it and would just call her in sick for the day.

Our mom's wounding wasn't letting her see my sister's pain because our mom was in so much pain herself. My sister didn't feel like she was even on their radar. Neither of my parents took an interest to go any deeper to see what was happening because they were wrapped up in their own dramas. They loved her, but they couldn't see what was going on with her. Later she found peace with our parents and has forgiven them and herself for the way things played out.

After earning my psychology degree, I moved to Chicago, worked in various fields, and experienced a lot of healing work. I eventually went back to graduate school and earned my master's degree and my professional license. Even as I was doing all this education and personal work, I still had a conflict between my idealized perfect self and my authentic self. I didn't know how disconnected I really was.

My life was new and exciting in Chicago. It looked functional, but I wasn't feeling functional. I was performing functional adult activities, such as holding a job, maintaining an apartment, and covering a car payment, but I felt all the cracks and wounds from more than two decades of absorbing and storing others' emotions. Between periods of learning to be a functional adult, my wounded self kept coming forward and making impulsive decisions.

At this point, in my mid-twenties, I was ready to break the illusion that I had had an ideal childhood, and I began therapy work that helped me grow from the inside out. I was tired of feeling less-than, confused, and having unfulfilling relationships. I knew something was wrong with me, but I didn't know what, and I certainly didn't have any tools in my toolbox to fix it. My therapist helped me to explore my adult self and understand how I learned to compensate and adapt to my life experiences. I began to understand how I brought all of my childhood wounding and emotional response tools into my adult life. It was through this therapy that I began to reconnect with my little boy self.

The first time I did inner child work was like pulling a dusty photo album off the shelf and turning the pages. The story was familiar, and even though I was looking at it more objectively through adult eyes, I experienced a resurgence of emotions from an earlier time. As I recalled the memories, I began to see the little boy inside of me who was smiling and happy on the outside but confused, scared, unhappy, angry, upset at himself, and lonely on the inside. As I told my therapist my story, though, I instinctively protected my mom and dad. I was propping them up on a pedestal and didn't want to dishonor or be disloyal to them. I didn't want to badmouth them to a total stranger.

We all know our parents made some poor choices, but we don't usually want to be mean; we want to protect them. This may be an attempt to keep them on a pedestal, to idealize them and our childhood. At some level we want to keep the illusion going, yet we also know that once we peek behind the curtain and shed light on what our childhood was really like, there is no going back. Keeping the illusion that everything was

OK even when we know it was not is our way of protecting the false self.

As I told my story about growing up and learning my wounded codependent traits, my therapist asked me how old little Bobby felt. I had never thought of that before, but it was easy for me to determine that this part of me was about ten years old, as this was the time in my life when things became highly reactive in our household. It felt intuitive to me that my ten-year-old self was carrying the collective wounding from this time period.

I came to understand that little Bobby was still very much within me, and when I was triggered in my adult life by something that felt chaotic, loud, angry, uncertain, out of control, weird, icky, mean, or threatening, little Bobby would become triggered and step forward. I was still living my emotional life through the eyes and feelings of a ten-year-old boy.

It became clear that I was coping and dealing with life emotionally as this little ten-year-old boy. As an adult I would get scared, shut down, overthink, internalize, and compensate for others' behaviors and choices. I would hold my feelings in, not show anyone my pain, and not let anyone in. Through my therapy I learned how to discern what was my emotional pain and what was someone else's pain. I learned how my wounded parts reacted to situations. I learned how to pay attention to my own attunement, to set boundaries, and to invite my authentic self to come forward.

From the outside I wanted to be seen as happy and successful—of course I did, because I wanted to be perfect for the outside world just like little Bobby wanted. I was struggling with self-acceptance, escaping to an unhappy job, and avoiding looking at my past. I wasn't living an authentic life; I was living as an adapted wounded child in a man's body.

My self-perception was reflected in the friendships I had developed. Apart from my childhood friends who were like brothers to me, some of the friends I had gathered around me in my early adult life in Chicago were what I call the "wounded birds": narcissistic, codependent, and dysfunctional, and in many cases also children of alcoholics. These friends reflected my codependent caretaker-rescuer-fixer self. They were the walking wounded just like me, but I thought I could help them, or at least relate to them. (Remember, hurt people find hurt people.) I was following the playbook of adult children of alcoholics. All of my wounded emotional response skills were the main characteristics of an adult child of an alcoholic: isolating, being overly responsible, caretaking, being needless, and focusing on others.

When I met people who were strong and authentic, I wondered how they did it. How were they so confident, and how did they know who they were? I could feel their inner strength. I wanted to be around them and would try to engage in friendship, but it never lasted long because I was not in a similar emotional space. It was as if I wanted to hang around them so some of their authenticity would rub off, but at the same time I didn't want to be around them because they didn't need my caretaking or fixing. I didn't know how to *be* with them because there was nothing for me to *do* for them.

Little Bobby didn't know how to be around or have friendships with others, especially men, who were confident, loud, rough, angry, or just guys being guys. It was scary and unpredictable for my little self, who thought that being loud and out of control and having big energy was too much like how my dad aggressively showed his emotions. I linked aggressive and even assertive male behavior to the trigger of being in an out-of-control situation.

As I healed my wounding, started to love and respect myself, and learned to set boundaries, my relationships improved. My outside world began to mirror my internal world, where I was beginning to feel strong, connected, authentic, free, and like myself. I was choosing to have others in my life who were living more authentically as I was living authentically. No longer was I making myself smaller for someone else's comfort.

As I healed, my relationships healed. I learned how to integrate my younger wounded parts into my functional adult self. I started using the functional response tools I had learned from my parents and others, such as giving myself permission to dream, creating what I wanted in life, and showing love and compassion to others and myself. I was no longer disconnected from my wounded little boy, because this part was healing. It wasn't getting triggered anymore, and my adult self was protecting all of me with healthy functional response tools, especially boundaries. Some of my friendships naturally faded away as my sense of self-worth grew stronger. As I set boundaries, my young adult friends who were around because I had always been there for them (but who never listened to me) no longer found me useful. I was seeing them for who they really were instead of who I wanted them to be. I learned how to respect myself, and I started emotionally cleaning house.

My mom and I always remained close, and as I got older and healed, I was able to have deep compassion and respect for her journey. I realized how much she sacrificed, albeit in an enabling way, in order to keep the family whole and intact for the greater good.

My relationship with my dad healed. I learned how to respect and love myself first, then I learned how to respect and love my dad for himself. I was able to fully accept and completely take in all of him to my heart. We were no longer me-against-him. I was able to forgive him for his shortcomings, his woundings, his anxieties, his drinking, his lashing out in pain. I was able to see his brightness, silent generosity, love, creativity, strength, and compassion. I was able to more clearly see both of us and how proud he was of me.

My parents have since passed away. I love and miss them all the time.

Part of our healing work is coming to terms with and accepting our past. The retelling of our stories can help this process of integration. We gain perspective about ourselves when we write and talk about our experiences. I wanted to share my story with you, as I will refer to it throughout the coming chapters as an example of core wounding and how the HEAL process can help you.

EXERCISE: WRITE YOUR THOUGHTS

Now that you have read my story, you may have some memories and feelings coming up. Take a few minutes to write them down in your notebook. How are parts of my story similar to your own? As you read my story, what feelings and memories were activated? Maybe you are seeing within yourself how you developed wounded emotional response tools to navigate your childhood family. Becoming aware of and writing down what you are feeling will help you when you do the timeline exercise in chapter 5.

THE MANY FORMS OF WOUNDING

Emotional trauma can come in many forms, from seemingly minor acts such as being yelled at to major events such as being in a car accident, living through an act of war, dealing with the death of a loved one, experiencing sexual abuse, and suffering mental cruelty. Trauma in any form has a lasting effect on us. The body, mind, and spirit go through a complex series of procedures to protect the core self and safely store core emotions during a traumatic event.

We navigate through trauma in three primary ways: suppression, repression, and dissociation. *Suppression* is when we consciously put a memory out of our minds. We actively choose to forget about it and don't give it any power. *Repression* happens when we unconsciously put out of our minds over a period of time an event that is painful for us to remember. *Dissociation* occurs during severe trauma, when the child's natural survival instinct says *you can try to hurt me, but you are not getting at my core.* The child or adult will internally disconnect from the event as a way of self-preservation.

After a trauma, the traumatized person doesn't always know that the event is over. This becomes the recycled pain that keeps trying to get our attention so that we do something about it.

Giving trauma a name is important because doing so takes the trauma out of the shadows. When traumas live in the dark, they become dark, dirty secrets. When traumas are not talked about and emotionally processed, they can run our lives. But when we name it, we can claim it.

Core Wounding

Core wounding sounds deeply painful, like a gaping sore or a wound from a traumatic event or memory that cuts deep. Emotional core wounding results from repeated small interactions with members of our family, as in my story, or those in whom we trust. These interactions can be small verbal jabs or snide or shameful remarks meant to hurt. They may happen once in a while or every day. Whatever the case, these are woundings that consistently show up. As they occur, we get used to these emotional hits. Eventually, they create a sore spot that develops into an invisible wound. This wound holds the frozen emotional pain, and it eventually becomes a part of us and informs our idea of self.

You may be thinking of events from your own life right now and wondering if what you experienced were core woundings. Each of us experienced hurt, disappointment, and shame growing up, yet many of these wounding experiences are a normal part of development and the human experience. They are not good or bad things, they just are. What makes the difference is how we are individually affected by these wounding experiences and how we navigate them, especially during childhood, when we were relying on our resilience and unique self-attunement.

Certainly, children who behave badly or are out of control with their emotions need to be corrected and disciplined. The error many parents make is to say that their *child* is bad rather than the *behavior*. Over time, the child connects this shame or ridicule as a negative statement about who they are at their core, forming a core wounding belief. The simple distinction between clarifying a bad child and bad behavior could have made many people's perceptions of themselves very different and changed the course of their lives.

Some of these wounding interactions we take in deeply, and others we just observe and move on. Look at your life and see what things deeply affected you. Were you told you were bad, or were you told that your behavior was bad? There is a big difference in how we take in and process these two types of emotional information.

Emotionally Frozen Wounds

When you experience a core wounding, it freezes at the age you were when you received the wounding, your *age of wounding*. This wounding stays frozen in time like a snow globe, and shows up again when it is triggered in your adult life. These frozen emotions and hurts do not progress chronologically with the rest of you, and the trauma or emotional pain is dormant until it is triggered, and then the cycle happens again.

This idea of a wound frozen in time and stuck in a snow globe inside of you is one way to understand and connect to that part of you that carries the wounding. It is a way to see yourself and the emotional pain you have carried for a long time from a different perspective.

Deep Trauma Wounding

Traumatic core wounding comes from a wounding that cuts extremely deep. Examples of deep trauma wounding include physical abuse, such as being hit, punched, and slapped; emotional abuse, such as being called names, feeling neglected, and not feeling wanted or honored; and sexual abuse, such as being forced to endure nonconsensual sex, being introduced to sex or porn at a young age, and seeing someone nonconsensually expose themselves. (Of course, this is not a comprehensive list.) These types of physical, mental, sexual, and emotional woundings, especially sexual abuse traumas, have a long-lasting effect and are deeply damaging.

All extremely traumatic wounding goes very deep into the psyche, and often takes longer to work through. This type of wounding often re-routes the emotional and intellectual development and initiates lifelong cycles of depression, anxiety, and even severe mental illness. Each of us has our own resilience to how we react, respond, and integrate these types of trauma.

Over the course of my career I have worked with individuals who have had such horrible things done to them that I have chosen not to use their stories as examples. I am deeply humbled to hear them, and I have tremendous compassion for them, knowing they had to endure such trauma as children. These extremely traumatic experiences stretch a person beyond their capacity, and we see them barely holding on, trying to live their life the best they can with the pain they carry.

Young children have a phenomenal ability to withstand the nuclear blast of an adult's rage and to develop adaptive skills to survive, both mentally and physically. I have seen both children and adults utilize their resilience to protect their authentic selves from harm, but we all have a breaking point of how much we can take, how much resilience we can call upon. The more trauma a person experiences over the course of their lifetime, the less they have in their resilience bank.

How we experience trauma is relative to the individual, so what may be devastating to one person can be a non-event to another. We each bring our worldview, personality, and sense of self into any situation we encounter. Some of us can weather a particular storm better than others.

People sometimes discount or minimize an event by thinking, *Well, everybody got spanked then* or *I was a bad kid, so I guess I deserved it.* Such rationalizations or minimizations help the mind make sense of or intellectualize the event so we can move past it. The mind consciously suppresses this and says, *Let's just move on, because I know if I stay in this emotional neighborhood much longer, I'm going to start to feel things I don't want to feel.* Move on, nothing to see here . . .

> If you were deeply traumatized by physical or sexual abuse, please know the following:
>
> - Abuse was something that was done *to you.*
> - *Nothing* you did caused the other person to do it to you.
> - It is not happening to you today. You are safe now.
> - You can get help and heal this wounding.
> - You can heal and embrace an authentic life.

Your relationship to your trauma needs to heal on your own time and at your own pace. You were not in control when the trauma occurred. You were physically smaller, you didn't have all the words you needed to express and protect yourself, and your world was literally a few blocks big. You relied on the adults in your life to keep you safe from all types of harm, but perhaps they were preoccupied with their own pain of addiction, mental illness, emotional distress, were working hard and didn't have time for you, or were themselves abused.

Sometimes a parent learns years later that their child experienced some kind of abuse and is filled with guilt. Either they didn't know or they turned a blind eye and minimized the situation, or the child was sworn to secrecy by the abuser to never tell anyone. If the parent is in emotional pain from their own wounding, they may not notice, understand, or see the child's emotional pain. Even though the parents are physically adults, they are probably much younger emotionally, and this shows up in how they respond or don't respond to their child.

Until we heal our wounding, we don't have the healed perspective to see other people's emotional wounds. It all feels normal, and "that's just how it is." For example, when a parent does not notice that their child is crying or distressed, the parent may have their own level of distress, and they need the same validation, nurturing, and care that the child needs. This is why emotional trauma within a family transfers from one generation to the next. The family as a whole is stuck in their emotionally frozen drama until someone breaks out and heals the cycle.

The wounded emotional response tools and impulsive reactions that develop from severe traumatic wounding experiences are specific to the trauma. A child who is sexually abused often learns how to detach from their emotions and compartmentalize. This is the trauma survival skill of *dissociation*. This traumatized child has an unconscious reaction to the situation in order to protect their very core. *This older, bigger, stronger person has more power and control than I do. They are doing something that is wrong, bad, and feels icky. They told me not to tell anyone. I've tried to say no, to fight back, but they are stronger and bigger than me, and they tell me I can't do anything about it. I feel powerless, so I'm giving in. Since I can't fight them, I have to go within to save myself. I will bury my emotions, my core, my personality, my voice, and my spirit deep inside of me for safekeeping. I'm not going to let them get the true me. They can do whatever they want to do with my body, but they are not getting to me.*

Many men and women have expressed to me that they emotionally and mentally survived a traumatic sexual assault as a child through what they later learned is dissociation. The weight and burden of the trauma feels incredibly heavy for a young child. Their sense of self-worth, love, trust, and respect is shattered. They no longer feel they can trust themselves or their world. They are forever changed.

Childhood sexual assault is incredibly damaging to a child's psyche. This type of deep core wounding creates specific coping skills and wounded emotional response tools, some of which are never detected by others by design. A child who was assaulted desperately wants to be invisible, so they adapt and go under the radar. They disguise their true feelings of shame and anger. They become watchful or hypervigilant. They disconnect from their feelings to survive the experience. In doing so, they shut down parts of their functional emotional response system and become detached and unfeeling. If the experience was incredibly traumatic, they dissociate.

Emotional wounding happens over the course of time or in an instant. Our experience of this wounding is based on our sense of self, authenticity, boundaries, and resilience. Core wounding comes in many forms, such as an off handed remark that stings, patterns of chaos in the household, or severe and repeated abuse. Deep emotional traumas can cause psychological and psychic damage, which can take far more work to heal. Unless the core emotional woundings are addressed, they have the potential to lead to unhealed woundings in adulthood, and the wounding pattern keeps repeating. The unaddressed core wounding becomes lost in the quest to stay alert for a familiar threat. Until the wounding is acknowledged, it does not heal and emotionally mature.

We keep choosing people to be in our lives that complete or play out our emotional dramas because the unhealed core wounding is stuck in place. We don't always know it is bad, we just think this is how our life is. This buried subconscious pattern enables the age of wounding to remain lost, fixed, and frozen in a snow globe, waiting to be triggered and then jump in with wounded tools.

As you go through the HEAL process, take your time and be gentle with yourself as you explore your core woundings. If you are unsure whether something is a core wounding or not, it probably is. If it has stayed with you this long and you have an emotional reaction to it when you remember it, this means it has a message for you. The good news is that all woundings can be healed, and you can become a fully integrated and whole adult through the HEAL process.

CHAPTER 4

Wounded Child, Wounded Adult

Out beyond ideas of wrongdoing and rightdoing there is a field.
I'll meet you there.

—RUMI

As we grow into adulthood we believe that we leave our childish behaviors behind. We interact with other adults, make adult decisions, and hold more responsibilities. But emotionally wounded children become emotionally wounded adults. Even as adults, we sometimes react impulsively to external events and are later embarrassed or ashamed by our behavior.

After the storm has cleared and emotions are calmer, the responsible adult self will assess the damage and think, *That didn't feel like me. Why would I act out in that way?* We are often confused after acting out. It doesn't make sense. We understand what we did, but we don't know why. The memory of the event is coated in shame, and we often can't imagine forgiving ourselves because the shame is so loud.

You do not have to live with this shame, and you can break the pattern of impulsive reactions. But until your core wounding is healed, you will carry around your wounded and lost inner child everywhere you go, vulnerable to inappropriate and impulsive reactions coming from your lost inner child at any time.

In this chapter you will begin the deep dive into the HEAL process. You will better understand why core wounding happens and how to heal the lost inner child so that it can integrate with the adult self. Once the core wounding is healed, it will no longer be triggered, and you will no longer repeat the same unhealthy patterns over and over. The wounded child will no longer control the wounded adult. This part will integrate with the responsible adult self, bringing a calm, peace, and freedom you may have never known.

REPEATING PATTERNS

People who seek to develop healthy relationships are often frustrated because they know at some level they are using outdated emotional responses and repeating the same patterns, but don't know what else to do. They earnestly want to move on from the pattern of getting in bad and unfulfilling relationships, but they haven't healed their emotional wounding. They have what I call a "bad picker," where they consistently pick partners based on their unacknowledged core woundings. This is another version of hurt people finding other hurt people. They say they don't want to be with someone like their ex, but then they start dating another version of that person. The new person may look and act differently, but the dynamic is essentially the same, and the person who wants to change will still use the same impulsive reactions in this relationship as they did in the last.

Their unhealed emotional wounding is looking for someone with whom to complete or play out the original wounded experience. At a deep level they want to heal the wounding pattern. They might subconsciously think, for example, *I really want to heal this hurt from my teenage boyfriend.* Their wounding then translates this desire internally with, *"Oh, I know, I will choose a narcissistic wounded person and be codependent with them, even though they will treat me poorly. It won't matter because I know how to adapt to that kind of situation—I have the tools.*

Of course we don't consciously think these things, but we do subconsciously. This is why some people will have a "bad picker" until they heal that part. They are picking partners based on their emotional wounding in an unconscious attempt to get past this relationship-replication cycle. Hurt people find hurt people, and healed people find healthy people.

Story: Bridget, a Forgotten Little Girl

Bridget has done well in her professional life, but her personal life has been challenging. She is divorced with two teenage boys, and shares parenting time with her ex-husband. When she first came to see me, she didn't have any interest in dating or getting close to anyone. When things were calm she felt OK, but most days she was disappointed, scared, and lonely.

When anything went wrong, or she got an unpleasant surprise, or her sons were driving her crazy, she would get really tense. Her core wounds would get triggered, causing her to become filled with rage and to verbally attack others. She used alcohol, pot, and prescription drugs to temporarily help her feel better.

Bridget recognized the recycled pain and wanted to stop the pattern. She didn't feel like herself when she was in an acting-out state. The feelings and behaviors she described were those of an upset child throwing a temper tantrum. This was not the language or action of her accomplished professional adult self; it was her wounded self lashing out at those closest to her.

Bridget identified her wounded inner child as about four years old. Early in her therapy, she hated the fact that she even had a wounded inner child. She learned through the HEAL process why this younger wounded part was showing up, but she was sick of the wounded part and the recycled pain. She said, "I just want her to go away! I hate her."

The HEAL process is not about ignoring or discarding the younger self, it is about integrating this part with the adult self. Bridget learned to identify the triggers that would set off the acting-out and how to develop a communication with this part of her. She created a list of her impulsive reactions so that she could identify when this emotionally frozen part of her was triggered.

One day, when she was mad at herself for even having this wounded inner child, I asked her what it was like where that little girl self lived inside of her. She stated without hesitation, "It is a cold, dark place with rags on the floor and no windows." "That sounds miserable," I said. I asked her what she would do if a four-year-old girl were standing in front of her feeling all these feelings and living in such a place. Bridget said that she would hug her and clean her up and get her to a better place to live. With this, she imagined a loving place for her little girl, with windows and no rags on the floor. By personifying this part of herself, she was able to stop rejecting the part that she most needed to embrace.

When her wounded little girl got triggered, Bridget felt

nervous, antsy, wary, and controlling. She created functional tools to use when this part shows up. We came up with words her responsible adult self could say, such as, "It's OK, I'm going to make sure nothing bad is going to happen. I am calm, and I trust myself to do the right thing." This was all she needed to say for her wounded self to be reassured and calmed. The more she set these internal boundaries with herself and external boundaries with others, the more her younger self knew that her responsible adult self was in charge.

Today Bridget continues to work on setting boundaries with herself and others. Her life isn't perfect; her boys still drive her nuts, and she is not dating anyone, but that younger part of her is no longer as impulsive and reactive. She works hard to recognize when her wounded parts show up, and she uses her functional response tools to give herself encouragement, reassurance, and self-love, knowing that this keeps her as grounded and authentic as she can be.

YOUR IMPULSIVE REACTION TOOLS

As you learned in chapter 1, you developed impulsive reaction tools in childhood in order to cope with your family situation and environment. You looked at some of the impulsive reaction tools you developed when you were a child (see "Exercise: Your Impulsive Reactions" in chapter 1). We are now going to honor these tools and examine them more deeply.

Honoring your impulsive reaction tools may seem counterintuitive, but they helped you adapt, respond, navigate, and make sense of the hurt, pain, and confusion when you were young. You used these wounded tools, now all battered and worn, to try to make life more manageable. Based on everything you knew of your world at the time, these tools were the best ones for the job.

The work you are doing here is one of self-love, not self-hatred or rejection. You can still use your impulsive tools, but now you will want to begin to use tools that help you expand instead of contract into a smaller version of yourself. The goal is for you to consciously know all of the tools you have developed and then discern what tool you want to use for a specific situation.

Think of a wounded tool you use, and hold it in your mind. For example, perhaps you overcompensate and try too hard to please others. Thank this tool for being available when you needed it in the past, and then ask yourself if you still need it or if you just use it out of habit. Can you put it down for now? Can you heal it and let it go? You may start to feel something stirring deep within. This is normal. Let this emotion wash over you like a storm going across a valley. It is just a storm, just a feeling. Let it pass over you and move on.

You may not be ready to give up a wounded tool that you have relied on for a long time because you don't know if you are going to need it again. This is a valid point, and in therapy we don't want to expose someone emotionally until they feel safe and know how to protect themselves. If you think you still need this tool, don't give it up. Just acknowledge this, and become conscious of when you are using it. I can still access my wounded tools if I want to, but I also know the price I pay in my relationships if I use an impulsive reaction tool instead of a functional tool.

Your emotional response tools, both impulsive and functional, are always available for you to use. Going forward, you will be asking yourself, *Is this the best tool for me to use right now?*

EXERCISE: HOW YOUR IMPULSIVE REACTION TOOLS DEVELOPED

This exercise is a continuation of the exercise you did in chapter 1, "Your Impulsive Reactions." Before you start this exercise, please review the list of impulsive reaction tools you wrote down in your notebook for the earlier exercise.

To give you an example of how to work through this exercise, let's use the impulsive reaction tool of, *I yell at others when I feel out of control*. If this is one of your impulsive tools, ask yourself why you needed that tool in your early life. For example, *I needed this tool to fight back when I felt defenseless*. Think about what, where, why, and who you created this impulsive reaction tool for. Think about the times you felt helpless, uncertain, scared, and worried. For example, *I created this tool as my defense when my older brother would beat me up*. Write down your answers next to each impulsive tool.

You can also write down who you learned the tool from, if this applies. Was it in response to something going on in your life or to what someone said or did to you? Did you see someone else doing it, or was it something that was put on you? A common thought during this exercise is, *I don't know why. I have just always done it this way*. That is fine. Write this down, too. We are so familiar with ourselves that even our dysfunctional actions and reactions feel normal.

Once you have your answers, carefully look them over as a whole. Do you see any repeating patterns? Write them down. For example, you may discover the pattern of choosing partners who you give power to or who behave as though they have power over you. Once you have identified a pattern, think about how it applies to your past and current relationships. <u>Do you think you choose friends or partners based on this pattern?</u> How is this related to your impulsive reaction tools?

This exercise is to help you begin to understand that you learned your emotionally wounded responses for a reason. You weren't born with these wounded tools; you created and developed them to help you cope. As you move through the HEAL process, you will discern whether or not these tools still serve you and whether or not you want to keep using them.

Set your results from this exercise aside for now. We will come back to them in chapter 5.

Broken Boundaries

Most people don't know whether or not they have good boundaries. They don't know how or even if they set boundaries and what it looks like. Boundaries create a sense of emotional safety in our relationships. They are our gut reaction to a situation, how we immediately feel when we like or dislike something or someone, or whether we want to do an activity or not. Our wounding will show up where and when we do not have healthy internal and external boundaries in place. When we have broken or fuzzy boundaries, our impulsive reactions play out in various ways throughout our adult lives.

When the lost inner child who doesn't have good boundaries reacts impulsively to a situation or event, the responsible adult self has to negotiate and manage the drama the wounded part creates. This lack of boundary setting creates a lot of confusion, and we can get lost in these dramas and in the loudness of our wounded parts. It is hard for the adult self to ignore this internal chaos and upheaval. Until healing happens and the adult self learns how to establish healthy, functional boundaries, the wounded self will continue to go back to the playbook and safety of the frozen emotions and impulsive reactions.

No Boundaries

A no-boundary situation is when we have not established a clear boundary statement of how we feel about something or someone, and we don't know how to assert ourselves with others using a boundary voice. People become *enmeshed* when they have a fuzzy idea of boundaries. They are often involved in everyone else's business, feel compelled to volunteer for everything, and let their friends and family dump their problems on them. In codependent terms they are the fixer, the rescuer, the controller. They often feel overwhelmed and don't know what to do with all of their own problems, so they start to meddle in other people's problems. *Enmeshment* is having fuzzy boundaries sometimes and no boundaries at other times.

People with no boundaries feel needless and wantless. They have learned to shut down and not claim any of their power, often acting as a victim instead. They don't know what they like or don't like, so they will ask others what *they* like and then copy that. They are fixated with others' behaviors and feelings. "What do you want?" "I don't know, what do you want?"

No-boundary people are often worn out from the lack of boundaries and the resulting enmeshment, and want to just run away from all of the drama that they attract and participate in. They have deep insecurities and a lifetime of letting others dictate who they should be and how they should think about themselves. They project their sense of right or wrong onto everyone else, which creates two major wounding patterns for the no-boundary person.

The first pattern is that of *mind reading*, or an attempt to imagine what someone else thinks and feels about them. This type of wounding is confusing for both people in a relationship. The person who is mind reading often makes up a story based on a few facts and then creates a scenario for what is probably happening. They project their insecurities and judgments onto the other person and make up stories that fit their idea of who or what the other person is thinking or feeling. Mind reading can quickly derail someone into thinking their life is a mess and everyone hates them.

The other pattern is the no-boundaries person passive-aggressively attempting to control others because they feel that others are trying to control them. The no-boundaries person tries to establish safety and control in relationships but does so indirectly, avoiding conflict and being sneaky. The no-boundaries person doesn't know how to talk about their feelings, so they hope the other person just gets the message from their avoidance, snide remarks, or doing things without asking. At first, the other person is oblivious to this and does not pick up on these subtle or indirect clues. This is especially true if the other person is narcissistically inclined. But most people know in time when they are being manipulated, and resentment sets in, further complicating the relationship.

> *Don't underestimate me and assume*
> *how I'm going to react.*

The no-boundaries person usually feels lost, resentful, stressed, tired, worried, and confused and doesn't know how they got this way. This behavior grows out of a sense of fear—fear of conflict, fear of being left out, fear of being unable to control a situation, fear that they are not involved or that they won't be needed. They are fearful of not being of value to the other person at all times and in all situations.

They are fearful of not having value to themselves, that they are literally worth less. People with no boundaries have lost themselves and usually experience a lot of sadness, drama, and hurt feelings.

EXERCISE: NO BOUNDARIES AND/OR ENMESHMENT

Do you think you have little or no boundaries with others? Do you think you might be enmeshed with family members or friends as a result? Having *no boundaries* means that you aren't paying any attention to what is OK and not OK for you to do, think, or have others do to you. *Enmeshment* is having flexible and fuzzy boundaries with ourselves and others, when you are in everyone else's business. It can be difficult to look inward at this part of yourself, but looking at your ability to set or not set boundaries is an important step toward creating a sense of safety for the wounded part inside.

Carefully consider the following questions, and write out the ones that have meaning for you. As you do so, just observe, don't condemn yourself. There is no right or wrong; you are just exploring where you are right now with your boundaries. You will use these answers when you learn to set healthy boundaries in chapter 6, so please keep them for later.

- Do I let others walk all over me?
- Do I play the victim? If so, why do I give others power over me?
- Do I want to run away because I am exhausted from trying to do everything for everyone?
- Do I wish that others could read my mind and just know what I need?

- Do I say to myself, *If they loved me, they would know what I need?*
- Do I test others to see how much they love me?
- Do I try to control others indirectly?
- Do I hope that others will pick up on clues when I feel angry, sad, or frustrated?
- Do I want to be invisible but seen at the same time?
- Do I let others dictate how I feel or how I should feel about myself?
- Do I think others are talking about me behind my back?
- Do I need to know what everyone else is doing?
- Do I give others my opinion even if they don't want it?
- Do I let others determine my reality because I don't know what I want?
- Do I feel unworthy to set boundaries or say no to others?
- Do I feel that I don't deserve anything?
- Do I try to help others with their lives because mine is a mess?
- Do I avoid taking ownership for anything?
- Do I disrespect what others think or believe?
- Do I doubt and question everyone?
- Do I doubt and question myself?

Look over the list of questions you answered yes to. Do you see any trends? These thoughts and behaviors are how your lack of boundaries and enmeshment show up in your relationships. They are a reflection of the healing work that is needed; they are not good or bad, they just are.

Let's go a little deeper with some questions about why you have a difficult time setting boundaries. Feel free to expand on these answers in your notebook. Be as honest as you can with yourself. Remember, this work is just for you unless you wish to share it.

- Have I tried to have a sense of power or to set boundaries in my relationships but gave up when it didn't work? (*They didn't like me saying no, so this didn't work. I will just agree with them from now on.*)
- Do I have a sense of whether people are good for me or toxic? Is it hard for me to see the distinction?
- Have I honestly examined if I play the victim role in my relationships? (*Poor me.*)
- Do I blame others or the situation and avoid taking responsibility for my actions?
- Do I know what is important to me, or do I just follow the leader and those who I think are better than me?
- Do I just want everybody to get along and not get into all of this drama? (*Magical thinking.*)
- Am I concerned that if I set boundaries, some people will not want to be in a relationship with me because I no longer cater to them?
- Have I created a list of my *wants* and *needs*?
- Have I actively tried taking care of myself?
- Have I honestly tried to not be involved in someone else's life as a distraction to my own? (*Am I preoccupied with others so I don't have to look at myself?*)

Your answers to these questions will help you begin to look at the patterns and themes that repeatedly show up in your life. If you need help creating a list of your needs, please see the Needs Inventory in appendix B.

Woundings keep recycling because of a poor or weak boundary system. Once you know how to set strong, functional boundaries, you will be able to reclaim your personal power and connect to your authentic self. You will be able to stop the cycle because you will know how to protect yourself in a functional way. The patterns and themes you are discovering through these exercises have contributed a lot of information to your narrative, and they shape your interior world (your self-talk and perception) more than you know.

Be gentle with yourself as you learn the art of boundary setting. You can find your boundary voice and create loving, mutually respectful relationships.

Setting healthy boundaries forms the exit strategies for our dysfunctional and toxic relationships. It also helps to redefine relationships that may have lost their way.

Bubble Boundaries

Many people walk around with an emotional suit of armor on, prepared at all times for an imaginary battle. The wounded part of them doesn't know that the battle is over, so they suit up every day with their wounded burden. They have what I call a *bubble boundary* around them to protect themselves from the world.

A bubble boundary is strong but fragile, malleable but rigid. It is the boundary you have when you hold people at arm's length, when you feel simultaneously guarded and open. It is neither extreme nor enmeshed. You participate in life and enjoy being with other people, yet you clench your teeth hoping they don't get too close. When you are in your bubble you feel protected; you can still see others and even let them get close, but you know in a millisecond when they get too close and touch your bubble boundary. Your bubble boundary is your sanctuary.

People with bubble boundaries learned to protect themselves from a childhood family where attacks came in the form of sly, passive-aggressive comments or deafening silence. There may have been very little expression or modeling of emotion in the household, so they never learned how to show their feelings.

Because of this lack of healthy emotional availability, these children grow up emotionally neglected and make up stories to make sense of their world. Basic needs such as food, clothing, and shelter were met, but emotional nourishment and nurturing went unfulfilled.

Sometimes this deficit of emotional expression and nurturing creates a void inside that the child tries to fill in other ways to make themselves feel whole. This behavior can come in the form of escapism, isolating, withdrawing, having a fantasy life, taking drugs or alcohol, self-harming, yelling, and other acting-out behaviors. These behaviors are emotional response tools that the wounded, lost inner child uses to self-soothe, cope, and make sense of their world. The child and parent fail to create a secure attachment bonding, which sets the child up for unhealthy attachment styles later in life.

Often in *emotionally unavailable* households the only communication the child receives is criticism or shaming, so they learn to keep their head down and stay low. At some point, they stop looking for parental emotional nourishment, and the wounded inner child retreats to an interior world and uses their wounded emotional response tools for protection, comfort, and reassurance. Over time, this boundary becomes a bubble surrounding and protecting them, but it was created out of confusion, frustration, necessity, and a place of lack. It doesn't align with their authentic self and their hopes and dreams for their life.

The ultimate forms of bubble boundaries are addiction, excessive drinking, inappropriate sex, drugs, keeping people at arm's length, and distractions from doing inner work. The short-term effect is numbing, but these behaviors eventually become crutches and then ineffective boundaries, all created to support the wounded narrative of the lost inner child.

The adult with a bubble boundary seeks out emotionally unavailable partners to replay this drama, repeating what they know in an attempt to feel loved. They want closeness, but they push people away. They secretly hope that someone will be able to see past their façade, through their bubble, to their real, wounded self, which is crying out for validation and love.

Sometimes, out of frustration, people with bubble boundaries will want to drop their stiff-arming, break the bubble, and open themselves up to a relationship. They want to feel connected and think that they can simply break their bubble boundary and become highly vulnerable, but this is too much, too soon. They don't always have a good "picker" when finding an intimate or romantic partner, and in their hasty attempt to achieve an intimate connection with someone, they sacrifice their own sense of self, which can have devastating consequences. They often have low self-esteem and don't feel that they are good enough, so they don't have strong functional boundary tools to back up and support themselves in such interactions.

The person who wants to suddenly break their bubble boundary can feel excited and nervous when meeting someone new. They might decide to tell all of their secrets and provide way too much information, putting all of their dirty laundry on the table. They subconsciously think that if they do so, the other person will know who they are right up front. They want to see if they draw the other person closer or push them away if they show who they really. They go from the known safety of a bubble boundary to having no boundary.

Since they don't know themselves emotionally and don't have a healthy boundary system, this oversharing is their attempt at creating intimacy, but it is also a test. Emotional dumping often overwhelms the other person and chases them away, which leaves the oversharer feeling the exposed shame of having revealed too much too soon. They feel foolish and retreat back into the sealed-off world inside their bubble.

Extreme Boundaries

Extreme boundaries are the opposite of no boundaries and much harsher than bubble boundaries. An *extreme boundary* involves making a dramatic life change that the person believes is the only way they can keep themselves emotionally, physically, mentally, or sexually safe from another person. An example of an extreme boundary is when someone moves to a different state or country to get away from another person or a family. Constructing such a boundary is like building a reinforced concrete fortress: it will keep others out for good.

People who establish extreme boundaries are usually angry and hurt from something someone else did to them, or they feel a great deal of fear about something. They are willing to walk away from a friendship, relationship, or work environment as a response to the fear they feel. They perceive that there are no other alternatives and that the only way to protect themselves is to shut out the other person or situation. Most people, however, establish extreme boundaries too quickly and out of a sense of frustration rather than a fear of being harmed. This happens when they don't know how to establish healthy boundaries.

Some examples of extreme boundaries are:

- I am moving away and not telling you where I am going.
- I am blocking you from all contact, including phone and social media.
- I won't acknowledge you even when we are in the same room.
- I will say no to everything and shut out everyone.
- I am not going to acknowledge my pain. I will shut myself off from myself. (This is an example of an extreme internal boundary.)

Some of these extreme nonfunctional boundaries might sound like they would be set by someone who needs to move a thousand miles away for their own protection, and some people do need to move away or block someone from their life for their own safety. (If this is the case for you, please see Resources in appendix C.) However, extreme boundaries need to be carefully considered and are a last resort because of the potential long-term damage they can create in a relationship connection.

If you are tempted to create an extreme boundary with someone in your life, ask yourself the following questions to determine whether this is the best option for you. Write down the answers in your notebook, and keep them handy for the boundary work in chapter 6.

Before you set an extreme boundary, ask yourself:

- Have I examined my feelings from a place of being grounded and not overly emotional? How do I feel as a result of what this person did or is doing to me? Do I need to set an extreme boundary, or is there a functional boundary I can establish?
- Have I expressed my boundaries with this person? Have I tried multiple times to engage with them or to meet up emotionally and talk things through? Have I tried my best to make this work with functional boundaries?

- Do I feel that no matter how clearly I express my boundaries, the other person does not respect them? Do I feel abused and neglected? Are my needs not being heard or respected?
- Have I considered the consequences of setting an extreme boundary with this person? How will I feel after I set an extreme boundary? What will the ramifications be on attempts to repair this relationship in the future?
- Do I have a clear sense of the other person's position? Am I making assumptions based on what they do or what they say they feel?
- Do I feel threatened in any way? If so, do I need to set an extreme boundary for my own safety and that of my family?
- Are my boundaries continually violated no matter what I say or do?

If you have answered these questions from a place of grounded clarity and still feel that you need an extreme boundary for personal and family protection, then proceed with caution and care. If you start to feel anger, spite, revenge, jealousy, and rage, then take a moment to re-center yourself. After you feel calmer, ask yourself if you need an extreme boundary or just need to work through your feelings. You want to feel grounded and centered when making such decisions.

If you can honestly answer from the bottom of your heart that you need to set an extreme boundary for self-protection and as a way to honor your sense of self-love, trust, and respect, then good for you for protecting yourself. But if you didn't give thought to the previous questions and want to shut down the relationship because it is too hard or messy to figure out, then you need to reexamine that and see if there is a more functional boundary for you to put into place.

Setting an extreme boundary without discerning the best approach will only perpetuate your wounding drama. People who set one extreme boundary will probably establish more of them with others because doing so is easier than working through the issues. This type of person often goes through life shutting lots of doors and leaving messy rooms filled with unfinished emotional business.

If you connect with any of the descriptions of missing, broken, bubble, or extreme boundaries we have been discussing, please remember that you also have healthy functional boundaries. Take a moment to consider the functional boundaries you have, the areas where you are doing a good job of maintaining your sense of self. These are relationships that feel balanced and reciprocal, where you feel honored, trusted, respected, and loved. These types of relationships are the gold standard to strive for when you are interacting with others and growing your connections. Many people have really good boundaries at work but poor boundaries at home. This is often the case because at work there are clearly defined rules of work and behavior, so people stay within the lines. At home, there are no work rules per se, so people tend to bring into their personal lives the boundaries or the lack thereof that they saw within their childhood family.

Remember, you are doing more things right than wrong. We are all doing our best with the tools we have, and as you work through the HEAL process, you are learning what is already working and what still needs some work.

Angry Boundaries

Many people will set a boundary with someone else only after they have had enough and become angry. They have been pushing down their feelings, and then they use the resulting pent-up anger and resentment to give themselves permission to stand up for themselves. They use the energy of stuffed emotion and their anger to justify the boundary. Later they can blame their anger as the reason why they set the boundary: "You made me so mad!" They hide behind this excuse and don't have to own their feelings. Recall that that is what I did at ten years old. I had stuffed my anger so much that I wasn't going to take it anymore. I was protecting my sister, and I was also at my breaking point.

Anger is fear under great pressure.

People who set boundaries out of anger are often not used to setting boundaries at all. They have a hard time expressing their feelings, so others don't know how they feel about something until they erupt in pent-up anger. They are told the problem is their anger, but that is not the problem. The problem is that they never learned what to do their natural anger, so now they stuff it and then explode.

Ironically, these are often the same people who received the message that the emotion of anger was bad or wrong to have at all, and thus the cycle of stuffing anger is seen more in men than women. Boys receive confusing mixed messages about emotions growing up: *Don't be angry, Don't cry, Tell me how you feel, I can't read your mind, Don't get into fights at school, You need to stand up for yourself, You're the man of the house now, man up!* Women and girls hear, *Don't be so emotional or dramatic, Why are you so quiet?, Tell me how you feel, You need to be strong to be taken seriously,* and they are under pressure to conform to society and make themselves smaller for the convenience of others while being told, *Just be yourself and love you for you.*

You never need to apologize, justify, or explain your feelings or your boundaries. Your feelings are your feelings. You have a choice in how you express anger. If your boundary has been violated, you don't need to have an excuse to tell someone what you are feeling; all you need to do is center yourself, find the emotion you are feeling, and give that wounded part a voice.

Using Feeling Words

Sometimes the hardest part of boundary setting is finding the right feeling word to describe the feeling. Once you have found the right word, then you can clearly express yourself. Suppose you feel hurt that someone didn't invite you to a party. Once you have identified the feeling of "hurt," you could say to that person, "I feel hurt that you did not invite me to go to that party." The other person may not know you feel this way—or they could have known what they were doing. Either way, the point is that you have spoken your heart's pain and are letting them know. You stood up for yourself, and you gave voice to the emotion you felt using the best feeling word.

When we don't say something, we are going to feel resentment about it later. We might even replay the situation over and over in our mind and continue to feel hurt—to recycle the pain. This is the body, mind, and spirit's way of telling us to deal with it. The longer we don't deal with a feeling, the louder it becomes within us.

When I was much younger and was first learning to express my feelings, I wasn't used to putting them into words, and I didn't have a big vocabulary to identify them. When I was really upset, I didn't know what to say or how to state a boundary, so, flustered, I would say, "I don't know how I feel. This just all feels weird and upsetting." These were not the most descriptive feeling words, but I was attempting to get my feelings heard. This is the important part, to get your feelings out in the most functional way you can, set a boundary, and go from there.

This practice is not about perfection, it is about honoring your feelings and giving them a voice. In time, your feelings vocabulary and usage will increase. If you have trouble finding a word that matches your mood, see the Feelings Chart in appendix A for an extensive list of feeling words.

SEVERE TRAUMA AND DISSOCIATION

As you have learned, a poor or nonexistent boundary system is often a result of a dysfunctional childhood family environment that was absent of healthy emotional response tools. Sadly, in many families the parents or guardians are so wounded themselves that they are not able to model any functional behaviors or boundaries, and they don't see or understand the emotional wounding that is happening to the child. The parents or guardians may even be the direct cause of traumatic wounding to the child. Because of this neglect, children in these circumstances have emotional woundings that go very deep and lead to devastating consequences in adulthood.

We have discussed how traumas are relative to each of us and how they coordinate with our own resilience and sense of self. Severe trauma, especially when repeated, can psychically, emotionally, and mentally damage a person to their core. While such trauma is happening, the person being traumatized often dissociates as a form of self-preservation. *You can do whatever you want to my body, but you are not going to get to my core.*

Dissociation is a trauma response that helps the traumatized person mentally and emotionally "check out" from the reality of the situation. To protect themselves, they unconsciously bury their essence and their feelings and prepare their minds to disconnect or go into a fantasy world as a preservation. This response is, in a sense, one of setting an internal extreme boundary, a retreat to safety that they can control. It is akin to their mental and emotional functioning going offline. They disconnect and go to another place in their mind while they wait out what is being done to them.

People who have PTSD will often dissociate when they are triggered. This can happen simply by having a conversation or seeing something on television that reminds them of the original trauma. They will mentally go somewhere else because this was how they coped when the initial trauma happened.

The unhealed traumatized brain doesn't always know if the trauma is over or not when a trigger occurs. When a person is triggered, they begin to watch their "trauma movie" in their mind's eye, usually from start to finish. Most people remember everything in a trauma memory in extreme detail: the surrounding sounds, touch, and emotion, whether it was a sunny or rainy day, what someone else was wearing, and what they smelled like.

I can recall every detail of taking my sister from the living room back to her room for safety, because it took all of my energy to make that happen and it was traumatic for me. Even though I don't have PTSD, I can recall everything from that event when I was ten years old. Not everyone who has a traumatic experience will be able to recall in detail what happened. Some people know something bad happened, but that is it.

If you feel something happened to you and you aren't sure, don't force yourself to recall this experience. When or if your subconscious is ready to release this information into your consciousness, that will be the time to process and heal the trauma. Forcing yourself to recall a memory can be just as traumatizing as the original event. Trust and know that if you are supposed to remember this, you will.

The following story is of a woman who experienced severe trauma in her early life and how her lack of boundary-setting skills as a child followed her into adulthood. She has been on a courageous journey, and you will see that it is possible to heal from a deeply traumatic childhood. You will learn how traumas that happened in childhood followed her into adulthood. It took courage, strength, and a willingness to slowly and lovingly acknowledge the pain and events that happened to her for her to heal. The story is difficult to read, but I include it to show you that people can heal their woundings, establish good boundaries, and become much healthier after a severely traumatic childhood.

Story: Marianne's Severe Childhood Trauma

As a child, Marianne was a good girl, but her mother saw her as always getting into trouble. She felt that no matter what she did she wasn't good enough. Her mother would send her to her room and tell her, "Wait until your father gets home." She learned to feel bad about herself, and would feel bad even when nothing bad was happening.

When Marianne was thirteen, a neighbor whom she trusted sexually molested her. When she told her mother, her mother didn't believe her. In fact, her mother never believed Marianne's stories of the abuse—or anything else, for that matter. She always doubted Marianne and was just generally not very nice to her. Being a smart girl, Marianne thought she just needed to try harder.

When she was sixteen, a teacher at her high school sexually assaulted her and told her not to tell anyone, but she bravely told the principal and her mother. Neither the principal nor her mother believed her; true to form, her mother again doubted her. Marianne learned to believe that others knew her better than she knew herself, even though none of it made any sense to her. She also learned to feel bad about and blame herself.

Marianne started acting out in school and talking back to her parents, primarily her mom. When she was seventeen, her parents, not knowing what else to do, admitted her to a mental hospital for three months because they saw *her* as the problem. While she was in the hospital, she met Mike, a male orderly who was older than she by six years. Mike charmed not only Marianne but also her mother. He told Marianne they were going to get married.

Mike and Marianne were married early in her senior year of high school. She thought she was marrying a charming man who was going to care for her, listen to her, and validate her, unlike her parents and the other men she encountered in her life. In time, however, she learned that her new husband was extremely narcissistic.

As with most narcissists, Mike's charm and kindness quickly went away. About nine months into their marriage, he became controlling and angry. He beat her up, and she would go to her mother, bloody and bruised, for help. Her mom would say that Marianne must have done something to make Mike angry, and that she should go back to him. Again her mother didn't believe her, and again she blamed herself. It was all her fault.

Over the course of their ten-year marriage, Mike continued to beat Marianne. He made her go to sex parties, where he forced her to have sex with other men and women and then tell him about it for his own sexual gratification. He would often threaten to kill her, and when he was driving the car, he would threaten to crash into a concrete barrier.

Anything could set him off. Marianne would make dinner for him, but he would find one thing wrong and break the serving dishes and plates on the floor and then make her clean it up. He told her she deserved it, and she believed him. He threatened her, beat her, and gaslighted her, manipulating her into thinking she was the crazy one. She suffered many more horrific events too numerous to detail.

She was in a violent domestic abuse situation and felt trapped. She told many people about the abuse, including doctors and clergy, but in the 1970s these professionals all turned a blind eye to abuse. They told her to stay with her husband and to try to make her marriage better, implying that her abuse was somehow her fault.

When Marianne was twenty-seven, she was finally able to leave Mike with the help of a man who truly loved her. She describes this man as her "lighthouse in a storm." Unfortunately, she had no capacity to receive or hold this man's love. She eventually left her rescuer, and in retrospect she is grateful that he helped her get out of the extremely abusive relationship with Mike.

Marianne's sense of self-worth, love, trust, and respect were beaten down, and she was exhausted from years of emotional, mental, physical, and sexual damage. She was among the walking wounded. Her story shows how her early childhood woundings and poor boundaries with both herself and her mother set the stage for her to be sexually assaulted and victimized. Her early experiences groomed her to be a target for an abusive narcissist in her adult life. But as with any child, she only knew what she knew, and she literally didn't know any better. She didn't know she had poor boundaries, she just thought her mother didn't listen to her. She tried to tell her emotionally unavailable mom all of this, but her mom also had poor boundaries and just blamed Marianne.

In his book *The Human Magnet Syndrome: The Codependent Narcissist Trap*, psychotherapist Ross Rosenberg writes about narcissistic abusers like Mike, who "possess an uncanny ability to discern whether potential victims are pathologically lonely or encumbered by core, real, or perceived beliefs of powerlessness and weakness. They seize upon anyone in a given crowd who appears isolated from others or whose loved ones, despite their protective and loving pronouncements, are uninterested in them and/or absent. The perfect [narcissistic abuse syndrome] victim has been taught the futility of fighting back, as doing so often makes matters worse."[1]

People will often read stories like Marianne's and wonder why people in such situations don't just leave, but people with low self-esteem and no boundaries don't see a clear path out. Marianne knew that how she was being treated was wrong. She tried getting help from adults to help her set boundaries, but her efforts to get assistance were continually thwarted. Her natural ability to protect herself became extinguished after repeated attempts. She began to believe she was the problem. In time, she felt she deserved this treatment, and she became lost in her own wounding.

When Marianne first came to me she was fifty-one years old, buttoned up, angrily defensive, controlling, a perfectionist, had major obsessive-compulsive behaviors, and felt only two emotions: anger and fear. She had daily symptoms of anxiety and depression, and kept acquaintances at work at arm's

---

1 Ross Rosenberg, *The Human Magnet Syndrome: The Codependent Narcissist Trap*, New York, Morgan James Publishing, 2019.

length. She could only set angry boundaries with others. Her physician recommended that she see me for therapy.

She was wary of talking to me, as she had told no one of what she had experienced as a child and young adult. After all, she had learned that telling her story didn't do any good. She had a profoundly disabled boundary system and had effectively established an extreme fortress-type boundary around herself. She had isolated herself from everyone else behind her armor and cut everyone out of her life.

Our work began very slowly, as I had to establish safety and earn her trust. I reassured her that we were going to go at her pace, in her own time, and that she was in control, because for much of her life she was not in control. She learned about the trauma response process and how her trauma response was natural for someone who had such an extensive PTSD wounding history.

Over our first few months of working together I saw how bright Marianne was and how she used her adaptive skills to not only survive the experiences but also channel her energy into her incredible mind's ability to organize data, manage complex transactions, and develop systems to manage compliance at work. I saw that behind Marianne's defensive anger she was a kind, thoughtful, and considerate person.

As our sessions progressed, I found myself repeating examples of how the body, mind, and spirit respond to trauma, but Marianne would react as if she had not heard them before. She was a bright woman, but she wasn't remembering what I had taught her about PTSD, trauma response, and coping skills. I finally realized that she was dissociating whenever she was triggered by a story she was telling me or when I referenced a story that reminded her of a trauma. She would look, act, and verbally respond normally as she carried on an intelligent conversation, but she wouldn't remember any of it later. She was dissociating and mentally replaying the trauma that corresponded to the trigger word, sound, story, or image that we were talking about. She had learned this wounded emotional response tool at a young age and was still using it decades later because it had served her so well.

Over time Marianne was able to recognize when she would begin to dissociate. I helped her to develop some grounding skills to keep her available and present. (With her feet on the floor, she would say, "I'm safe right now, I am in control. It's not happening to me now, and I trust myself to protect myself.") She began to recognize when she would dissociate at home, at the store, and out to lunch with friends. It was happening more than she realized, and she understood that she had to develop new functional response tools to help her become emotionally healthier.

Marianne learned to trust herself and listen to herself and her needs. She got a dog and felt unconditional love for the first time. She learned that she had been victimized by her perpetrators and that she wasn't the problem. She learned how to connect with others and develop friendships. She took self-help classes and began to love, trust, and respect herself. This self-love is still hard for her to accept, but she makes progress every day. If someone had believed her and believed in her when her traumas were happening, the course of the rest of her life would have had a very different outcome, and she would have a very different story.

Today Marianne still dissociates, but the triggers are usually connected to something she reads or sees in a movie or a show on TV. She is able to come out of the dissociated state, recognize what is happening, and move on. She still has obsessive-compulsive behaviors, but she sees them for what they are, and we monitor these occurrences and their frequency.

Marianne now uses her words to protect, express, and defend herself. She knows that if a situation feels bad or uncomfortable, she has the tools to protect herself, and she knows she has the power to leave. She chooses to have people in her life who honor her, and her relationships are reciprocal. Every day Marianne demonstrates the power of practicing good boundaries. She continues to use the HEAL process to embrace and transform her woundings.

(If you are a victim of abuse of any kind, please see Resources in appendix C.)

In this chapter you learned from others how their wounded child became a wounded adult. Discovering some of the reasons you carry emotional pain can be scary and overwhelming, but understanding your past is important so that you can know where you want to go in your future.

No one wants to remember painful memories if we think there is nothing we can do about it. Recognizing the strength, resilience, and perseverance you have demonstrated to get this far in life is your reminder that you are bigger and stronger than anything that has ever happened to you.

Marianne survived many deeply traumatic situations and then learned how to thrive and love herself. So can you.

CHAPTER 5

Applying the HEAL Process

The privilege of a lifetime is to be who we are.

—JOSEPH CAMPBELL

Healing your lost inner child wounding takes time, gentle care, and learning to love and embrace your wounded parts. In earlier chapters you learned about the wounded inner child, how wounding happens, how triggers affect the wounded child in adulthood, and how healing these wounds will allow you to live a healthier, happier life. You have been uncovering childhood memories and events that led to core woundings that still affect you today. You have learned about why you have impulsive reactions and what some of your emotional response tools are. All of this information and understanding is going to come into play now. The deep self-exploration you are about to do in this chapter will allow you to heal your inner woundings and embrace an authentic life.

The HEAL process is about creating links of trust and connection with all parts of yourself.

Before you start on this phase of the HEAL process, it is important that you set aside some common defenses that come up in this type of therapy. These fearful objections can derail the process and hold you back. To get the most out of this process, it is crucial that you recognize and consciously avoid the following defenses.

- **Discounting**—Set aside the temptation to discount or minimize the difficult or traumatic experiences you had growing up. In other words, don't normalize your emotional pain. ("It wasn't that bad".)
- **Normalizing the abnormal**—Resist the urge to make the abnormal normal. ("Everyone was beaten.")
- **Protecting others**—Resist the urge to protect your parents, guardians, family members, and others. This work is not about dishonoring them, it is about honoring yourself.
- **Denying that healing is possible**—Avoid the temptation to think you can't heal because you can't change the past. ("Why would I want to go back and look at that if I can't change it? What has happened, happened, and nothing can be done.")
- **Avoiding bad memories**—Let go of the idea that you can heal without exploring bad memories. It takes courage to heal, and you are worth it. ("I can't remember much of what happened, and what I do remember I don't like, so why go there?")

Many people don't want to look at their childhood woundings because doing so is painful. If you have this reaction, you may be compartmentalizing these painful experiences and pretending that things weren't that bad. *I turned out OK, didn't I?* Such rationalizations give you an excuse to avoid feeling or looking at things. However, as you have learned in earlier chapters, touching on the events you have experienced is not going to kill you. It may hurt or sting, but you are stronger than you know, and with some self-care you will get through this process intact and feel much better.

If you start feeling resistance to the work, know that this is a normal reaction. Acknowledge the defensive reaction, then give yourself permission to look at all aspects of your childhood to see how they feel to you today.

In the next section, you are going to create a timeline that will help put your early woundings and standout events in perspective. This living blueprint of your life will help you to see yourself and your life events from a different perspective.

The timeline focuses on your developmental years from birth to age twenty. Don't be concerned about keeping to this specific age range, as some people have deep, painful wounding experiences in their early twenties and even later, so this isn't a hard and fast rule. However, the earlier years tend to be when deep wounding or trauma impacts people the most, and this is when these lifelong wounding patterns become established.

The Childhood Timeline

Many people say that they don't remember a lot from when they were really young, and that is pretty common. Most of us do not recall many memories from the very young and toddler stages. However, when we are very young we do begin to develop two types of long-term memories: implicit and explicit. An *implicit memory* is one that is stored in the unconscious before the age of three. For example, you may not remember specific outings with Dad every Saturday morning, but you get a warm, emotional, fuzzy feeling whenever you think of being with him. At about three years old, *explicit memories* begin to be stored, such as consciously recalling Dad taking you out for breakfast every Saturday morning, where you went, and how you got there.

The majority of our memories up until the age of seven are implicit memories, but age three is the turning point when explicit memories become more frequent. Most people are able to recall events or situations from about age five and up. Starting at age seven, a child's memories are similar to that of an adult. If you have gaps in your memory, you may have used repression, suppression, or dissociation to cope with your feelings. The memories are there, but don't force them if they do not naturally surface into your consciousness.

Before you create your own timeline, let's look at an example.

Nicole is a thirty-year-old single woman who lives on her own. She feels closer to her dad than her mom, and has a younger brother with whom she is close. She has a professional job and a few close friends she meets for drinks. She is dating, but nothing too serious.

We can see in Nicole's timeline that some situations in her young life would be considered good events and others bad. She has included all of the events that stand out in her memory, describing each one in broad terms.

Age 3: Mom and Dad divorced

Age 5: Mom remarried; hard time emotionally

Age 6: Fun birthday party, all my friends were there

Age 7: Dad remarried; things got better

Age 8: Bullying in school started

Age 10: Met my best friend

Age 11: New middle school, had to leave my friends

Age 13: First crush

Age 15: First time to have sex

Age 16: Dad got really sick, almost died

Age 16: Wrecked the family car after getting license

Age 17: Bad grades at school; didn't want to be there, felt lost

Age 18: Graduated but had no direction

Age 19: In college, but it was really hard; started smoking pot and drinking

Age 20: Almost failed out of college

The descriptions are just enough to jog Nicole's memory and see some patterns. Let's look at some of those patterns and standout memories.

Five years old was hard because her parents were divorced and her mom remarried. Life settled down, but then things started to get bad again around age sixteen, when her dad almost died. At age seventeen she no longer wanted to be in school. She was not suicidal, she just didn't want to be in her life anymore. It felt like too much.

We can see that the wounding from Nicole's early years lands around the age of five, when she was having a hard time emotionally with her mom remarrying and a step-dad entering her life. She starting feeling lost around age seventeen. These two specific emotional standouts on her timeline, at ages five and seventeen, represent her *age of wounding*. She can focus first on the age of wounding that feels the "loudest" inside of her.

Creating Your Timeline

It is time to take a deep dive into your own timeline and identify your emotional standouts. Take your time with this process, and be gentle with yourself. Set aside plenty of time, and be in a place where you won't be disturbed or interrupted. You are about to do some deeply personal and important work. All of that said, do not overthink it. This is your story, and you know the details.

In your notebook, orient a blank sheet of paper horizontally. Draw a line across the middle from left to right, then make marks to denote the years between birth and age twenty. Read the next several paragraphs to see how to recall standout events, then start writing.

Be quiet and let your mind wander. Begin to picture the events of your past unfolding like a movie. As your mind flows, jot down some events that stand out. Write down short phrases along the timeline next to the age you were when each event occurred. Some people write out incredibly detailed memories, and others write brief notes. Do what works for you.

Avoid discounting events by thinking they weren't a big deal or that those things happened to everyone. That may be true, but it will all contribute to your understanding of yourself. Just let things come up. Continue writing these events on your timeline.

Some situations may be uncomfortable to think about, so for now just make a mark or write down just enough of a description to remind you later. Suppose you remember an event from when you were seven when someone touched you inappropriately and it felt icky. Just write down "icky." This work is not about resurfacing trauma just to get through the exercise, so be gentle with yourself as you go through this process.

If you have difficulty remembering events, it may help to talk with a trusted friend or relative who knew you before you were twenty. If you feel comfortable, tell them what you are doing and see if they have any insights into your early life. They might remember something about you that stands out for them but for you it was just another day.

Continue filling out your timeline. You may have more information to write down as you get into your teenage years, which is normal.

The Emotional Response Scale

Once you have filled in your timeline, you are ready to determine the level of intensity that each event holds for you using the Emotional Response Scale. This exercise will help you to better define how you feel about these events today. It is based on your subjective measurement, so honoring how you feel about each event is important. These ratings are going to help you determine your *age of wounding*.

The Emotional Response Scale uses a scale of 0 through 10, with 0 having the lowest emotional intensity (neutral, happy, or joyful) and 10 the highest emotional intensity (great shame or sadness). The scale is not used to rate an event as "good" or "bad." It simply rates the level of intensity inside of you when you recall the event.

You will be using the following descriptions of the Emotional Response Scale to determine the level of intensity of each standout event on your timeline.

Low Intensity (1 – 3)

Examples of a low intensity rating are:

- This event really bothered me as a kid, but the memory doesn't bother me now.
- I feel neutral most of the time when I remember this event.
- This event was happy and full of joy.
- I just shrug over this memory, and I can move on.
- I can be around the person who hurt me, I have forgiven them and let it go, and it is not a big deal anymore.
- I used to get really angry at this situation or person, but I have worked through the pain and have a greater perspective today.

Mid-Range Intensity (4 – 6)

Examples of a mid-range intensity rating are:

- I have seen pictures of a time when I know things weren't

good, but I look happy, so I am confused about how I "should" feel.

- Sometimes I am upset about what happened to me but not all the time.
- I can be around these people or situations sometimes but not all the time.
- This type of situation (family dynamic or chronic issue) still creates turmoil in my life; I don't like it and want it to go away.
- When I remember this event it stings, but the bad or shameful feeling comes and goes.

HIGH INTENSITY (7 – 10)

- I get really angry or feel hurt or sad whenever I think of what happened.
- I withdraw, get very quiet, and shut down whenever I think of what happened.
- I have a physical reaction if I am in a certain area or around people who remind me of my abuser.
- I am filled with shame and pain when I remember this event.
- I wish this memory would just go away. I want to erase the whole event.
- I dissociate or "zone out" when I think of this event or when I get triggered. (This is a level 10 intensity.)

Look over your timeline, and as you remember each situation, rate the intensity of the feeling between 0 and 10. Write this number down next to each event using a colored pen or pencil. This information is just for you, so be honest with yourself.

Once you have rated each event, sit back and look over your timeline again. What does this big picture tell you about your early life? Are there a lot of low- to mid-range ratings next to each event?

Or did you rate many of them mid- to high-intensity? What do the ratings reveal? Are the high-intensity ratings clumped together, or are they scattered throughout the timeline?

Remember that the ratings exercise is a way to measure the events of your life and to recognize that some situations were very intense. It can help you to determine an age of wounding that will help you to see the symptoms manifesting in your adult life.

Your Childhood Household

Another way to look at your timeline and the events that happened in your first two decades is to think of your childhood household and all of its members and what the interactions were like. The following are descriptions of how a household may have felt as it relates to the Emotional Response Scale, and how growing up in such a household may manifest emotionally and relationally in your adult life.

LOW-INTENSITY HOUSEHOLD

If you grew up in a household with an overall low-intensity rating, you probably felt good about yourself most of the time. There were situations that occurred now and then that upset you but nothing bizarre or odd. You were able to brush off most things that were unpleasant. You met and kept friends, and even though life wasn't perfect, you had more happy times than angry or hurtful times. Consistent, loving adults were always present. The adults had their own issues, but they could regulate their emotions and provide a flow of stable love and reflection back to you. You felt validated, honored, and cherished by the adults in your life. You still feel this feeling as a warm glow in your heart or belly when you think of specific times growing up.

How a Low-Intensity Household Experience May Manifest in Adult Life

As an adult, you are able to check in with your partner or friends when things are bothering you. The overall good feeling from your childhood experiences carries over into your adult experiences. Your adulthood mirrors the type of childhood and family environment that you had growing up.

MID-RANGE INTENSITY HOUSEHOLD

If you grew up in a household with an overall mid-range intensity rating, you probably feel that your home life was OK for the most part, but you didn't always feel OK. What was happening on the outside didn't always match the inside, like the beautiful house that the neighbors see doesn't always match what is going on behind closed doors. You felt puzzled about yourself and thought, *No one understands me* or *No one likes me*.

Growing up in a mid-range intensity household indicates that your childhood was not filled with big emotional or traumatic events that happened over and over, but at times the family could tip over into bad times. This is a childhood in which the hurtful or angry times could overshadow the happy times. There were adults who you felt were safe and in charge, but there were also those who frightened you, and you tried to stay away from them.

In a mid-range intensity household, alcohol, drugs, gambling, and other addictions may show up in parents, siblings, or other relatives.

How a Mid-Range Intensity Household Experience May Manifest in Adult Life

You came away from this type of childhood feeling more battle-scarred than your friends but generally OK. You feel good about yourself most of the time. You may take or have taken medications or therapy for anxiety or depression in your adult life, but this is, for the most part, not an ongoing need. You may be able to stay in a long-term relationship, but it will require work to make it functional, as many of your unresolved issues from childhood will be brought into your adult relationships.

HIGH-INTENSITY HOUSEHOLD

An overall high-intensity household indicates a childhood with consistent turmoil and upset. There may have been stable adults around, but this was not a constant. You were always searching for someone in charge, and if you couldn't find a grounded adult, then you felt like you had to be in charge and stay in control because everyone else was out of control. You often had physical issues such as headaches, gut issues, nervousness, and being hypervigilant. This watchful feeling would happen even when things were good because you were always waiting for the next explosion to happen.

Chaos, alcohol abuse, and multiple addictions by the parents or primary caregivers are often seen in this type of household. The caregivers were often lost in their own troubles and didn't have time for you. The first-born became super responsible, or the kids all checked out and looked for ways to escape.

How a High-Intensity Household Experience May Manifest in Adult Life

As an adult, you have tried therapy multiple times and have been on and off different types of medications in your desire to feel better. Your early life and adult life are confusing to you, and you wonder how other people are able to be happy. You have difficulty maintaining emotionally close connections with your partners, and you are drawn to the same type of person over and over even though you know they are not good for you. You may say you don't want the type of household you had growing up, but it seems like chaos is inevitable.

For example, I rated my age of wounding at ten years old, and rated my traumatic memory of getting my sister and myself to safety as high in intensity, at a level ten. I evaluated that my childhood family experience went from the mid- to high-intensity household range.

Look over your timeline, your intensity ratings, and these household descriptions. What patterns do you see? Do you see your childhood household experience from a different perspective? These intensity ratings help to illustrate and quantify your experiences so you can be objective with your own history. I include them as reference points so you know that you are not alone, that many others come from similar experiences.

You have been doing some difficult searching inside, probably looking at things you haven't thought about for a long time. At times this emotional excavation is really heavy, tiring, and overwhelming. We will continue to go even deeper, but for now, let's take a short break and give your emotions a rest.

EXERCISE: YOUR TREASURE CHEST

Our emotional treasures don't always sparkle.

I want to teach you a meditation and visualization technique that is useful for when you bring up emotionally heavy parts of your past, as you did in the last exercise.

Picture all of the things you have been thinking about from your childhood, all of the emotional wounding events that are in your conscious mind. Imagine these events scattered on the floor like little treasures. As you begin to connect to them, remember that you are discovering a lot of emotion that is packed within each situation.

Picture a treasure chest on the floor along with all of your scattered childhood memories. The treasure chest is the safe cocoon that will hold all of these emotionally laden events so you don't feel like you are walking around open and exposed, raw with emotion. It will magically expand to hold everything you will be putting into it.

Pick up and hold a memory, and thank it for being in your life. Even if it was painful to go through when you were younger, it is still a treasured part of you because all of you is treasured. Hold this memory, thank it, and place it in the treasure chest.

Continue to put your emotional memories into the treasure chest one by one until you have gathered them all. Once they are all in the chest, close the lid.

Put this treasure chest in a safe place inside of you. Know that when the time is right you will open it and gently bring out these emotional memories. In time, you will be healing the emotions that are wrapped around each of the more painful events, but for now, keep them in a safe place so you can begin to feel whole again as you do this healing work.

Emotional Standouts

Look at your timeline again and note the events that you rated between 7 and 10 on the Emotional Response Scale. These are the *emotional standouts* that have a high emotional intensity, the experiences that were difficult for you and impacted your life path. When you are triggered or remember these standouts, you remember them very clearly, and they really hurt. Use a highlighter to mark these emotional standouts on your timeline, or write them on another piece of paper.

Your Age of Wounding

In earlier chapters we touched on the *age of wounding*, a dramatic or emotionally significant event you experienced as a child that resulted in a core wounding. This wounding event gets linked with the age you were when it occurred, which results in the wounding becoming frozen in time, trapped in a snow globe within you.

Let's look at another example of determining the age of wounding. John's parents divorced when he was seven years old, but the upset and turmoil between his parents carried on until he was twelve. This five-year range was an emotionally difficult time in his life because he was constantly shuttled back and forth between their houses. He could not process everything that was happening when he was so young, and toward the end of the period he was entering puberty. He felt overwhelmed and confused.

John's emotional memory around the age of seven carried some heavy weight, as did the age of twelve. It was hard to say which felt more intense as he looked over his timeline. To pinpoint the age of wounding, John asked himself if the wounding from ages seven to twelve was at its worst at the beginning of this timeframe, with his parents' divorce when he was five, or when his mom remarried when he was twelve. He determined that it was most intense when his mom remarried. His dad, whom he was really close to, was pushed to the background, and now he had another man whom he had to call dad. On the surface it seems like the divorce would have been the hardest emotional part, but in fact it was when his mom remarried. The age of wounding of twelve was heavier on his heart.

To determine your age of wounding, look at your emotional

standouts—the high-intensity events on your timeline—and make note of your age or age range during those times. Your wounding may have a specific age, but you don't have to be precise. As with John's example, it could be a timeframe, such as seven to twelve years old. Physical, mental, emotional, or sexual abuse may have happened over a period of years or at one specific time. It is not important to get the exact age right, and in fact, if you had multiple periods of extreme situations in your young life, you may have multiple parts of you that carry this wounding.

Many people intuitively connect with an age that carries their wounding, but none of this is an exact science. If you determine that age five, for example, works for you at first but later in the process your age of wounding feels older or younger, then simply adjust it.

Be gentle with yourself through this entire process, as a lot of emotional residue will be stirred up. If you find that recalling these memories is too much for you, then seek professional help. Don't force yourself to remember the really bad stuff, and don't force yourself through the process. If something deeply traumatic did happen to you, know that *you are in control today*. When you were a child you were not in control of what was done to you, but today you are. *You* set the pace for how you go through this process.

> *You carry a unique wisdom about yourself*
> *that no one else possesses.*

You have a great wisdom because of your experiences. Know that you carry a light of emotional wisdom within you because you have been to some dark places within yourself, you have come out on the other side of these experiences, and now you know more. This wisdom helps you more than you may think. See if you can call on your inner wisdom to help guide you through this process of unfolding.

Other Ways to Find Your Age of Wounding

If you are having trouble identifying an age of wounding, don't worry; there are other ways to approach it. You can look at the feelings, behaviors, and wounded emotional response tools you use as an adult, and refer to that part to determine your age of wounding. You can recall from the stories you have read so far how the person's behaviors were those of a child's and how this often correlates to their age of wounding.

Sometimes when a client tells me about impulsively acting out, I ask them how old they feel. Every one of them is able to identify an age pretty quickly, such as, "I feel like a little kid when I yell and scream." I then ask them how old that little kid is inside. Or you might see that acting impulsively reminds you of when you were a teenager, for example. This is a reverse-engineering approach to identifying your impulsive part, your selfish part, your hurt part. It is another way to understand the emotional dynamics that keep showing up in your adult relationships and how they correspond to a younger age.

You can also turn to trusted people to help you determine your age of wounding and to help you see patterns and themes in your life, which we will explore next. Keep in mind that when you ask your friends about your life, you open yourself to being vulnerable, so be careful when doing so. If you do decide to open up to another, choose a close friend who will be gentle in their assessment of you and your patterns.

When you feel safe and secure, ask your friend the following questions:

- What do you often see me do that keeps me small and doesn't help me grow?
- What type of people do I gravitate toward?

- What type of people do I attract?
- How do you see me react to upsetting situations?
- What do you hear me say when I have big reactions?
- Do you see me giving away my power to other people?
- What do you often hear me talk about?
- Do I keep telling the same stories? Do I complain about certain things over and over?
- What do I tend to focus on and repeat?
- When I behave certain ways or make certain choices, how old do I sound to you?

This feedback can be hard to hear, but if you choose someone whom you trust and who knows you, they can give you some insight into yourself to help you narrow down your childhood wounding ages.

Suppose your friend says that you often act like a teenager. When you ask them to be more specific, they say you sometimes act like a fifteen-year-old. Look at your timeline and determine what was going on in your life at age fifteen. There are a lot of ways to go about getting to your age of wounding.

Remember that your friend's answers will be their own subjective measure or even a projection, but they may help you to clarify parts of your timeline or your triggering experiences as an adult.

Recurring Patterns

Now that you have your timeline filled out as much as you can remember, take a step back and look over what you have created. Do you notice any big gaps between ages? Are there certain ages where events are clustered together?

You may be starting to see patterns or themes pop out. What memories do you keep recycling? What is on your "highlight reel"?

What memories can't you forget, can't get past, or don't want to remember at all? Can you see a pattern to these memories?

Here are some examples of patterns you may notice from your timeline exercise:

- Feeling sad, lonely, isolated, not good enough, or misunderstood
- Attracting the same type of friends or relationships into your life (narcissistic or manipulative people whom you are always doing something for but who do not reciprocate)
- Feeling less-than; everyone else is superior
- Feeling left out, never included
- Feeling like the victim and blaming others for your pain
- Constantly seeking outside approval
- Getting angry and lashing out but feeling hurt inside
- Doubting yourself and giving others power

Notice the patterns or themes that your timeline reveals. They are clues to your healing path. Also look at the choices you keep making. What would your friends say about your patterns?

Look at the themes in your childhood family. Was your family respectful of boundaries? Did you feel close? Or was each person like an island, isolated from the rest? Did everyone do their own thing? Or was your family enmeshed, where everyone knew everything and got into everyone else's business?

> *When you feel triggered, something inside of you needs healing.*

You may find themes of abandonment or loneliness in your timeline. Or perhaps nothing relates, and you just experienced random events. However, if you look at these random events more deeply, you may see relationship dynamics or situations happening in your life now that are similar to situations from your childhood. You could even be in a relationship with the same type of person you were interested in when you were in high school. We are creatures of habit; it is easier to keep doing the same things over and over, even if they are not healthy for us.

You may have periods of dormancy in your timeline when nothing major happened. The dysfunctional family dance may have still been happening, but you were not being triggered to the point of having to defend yourself. All through this dormancy period, your wounded and functional emotional response tools were right by your side in case you needed them.

Maybe you were like me and had a parent who abused alcohol or were alcohol- or drug-dependent, and you learned to blank out big parts of your childhood. This self-protective measure helped us to cope during times that were overwhelming. It was our way of pushing away the memories of the feelings or events that were painful or hurtful. To this day there are sections of my childhood that I cannot recall, which most likely means I suppressed these memories even though I have seen pictures and know those experiences happened.

You have been doing some difficult work, and this is a good time to take a break. When we are reliving past events that are emotionally charged, we often hold our breath as a trauma response to determine what the threat is and whether or not we have to take quick action. We take shallow breaths in the upper chest, which reinforces the message to the body and mind that we need to be on alert and ready to fight, flee, or freeze.

The following exercise will help you to breathe more deeply, which in turn will relax your whole body. You can do it anywhere and anytime you need to tell your body, mind, and spirit system that it can relax, there is no threat, no one is running after you, and you can be still and quiet. I advise most people to do this exercise once an hour if they are really wound up.

EXERCISE: SIMPLE BREATH

This process rebalances your system and tells all parts of you that you are safe and there is no need to feel scared. Looking out at nature or listening to some relaxing music adds to the experience. Give yourself this gift of gentle breathing.

Sit comfortably in a quiet place. Close your eyes, place one hand on your belly, and take a long, slow breath in through your nose, then gently exhale through your mouth. Don't force it, just breathe gently in through your nose and out through your mouth, as if you are gently blowing out a candle. At first you may breathe faster than you need to, but just relax into the flow and go slowly.

If we really love ourselves, everything in our life works.

—LOUISE HAY

IDENTIFYING TRIGGERS

Triggers can be actions, words, people, and events that activate your impulsive reactions and cause your lost inner child to act out. Identifying these triggers is a way for you to connect to your core woundings. Now that you have determined your age of wounding, identifying your triggers will help you to know in real time when your emotional wounding is showing up in your adult life. You will then be able to choose mature responses that will help calm this part of you so that your responsible adult self can remain in control.

Triggers can come from sight, sound, smell, touch, or a situation. A trigger can be something or someone that immediately scares you, angers you, irritates you, offends you, disrespects you, minimizes you, discounts you, shames you, or ignores you.

EXERCISE: IDENTIFY YOUR TRIGGERS

Get out your notebook and look over your list of wounded emotional response tools that you identified in chapter 1 in "Exercise: Your Impulsive Reactions." Use this list to help you identify some of your triggers.

Think about a situation that upsets you, then write down your answers to the following questions in your notebook.

- When and where does this situation usually happen?
- Is this a sight, sound, smell, or touch?
- Is your trigger a person, a thing, or a situation?
- How often does it occur?
- What are some immediate feelings you have when this situation occurs? (I immediately feel . . .)
- Where do you feel this in your body?
- Do you find you want to say or do something, or do you want to be super quiet and withdraw?

- Are the same people or same type of people involved in this situation?
- Of whom or what does this situation remind you of from your early life?

Don't overthink your answers to these questions. Your first instinct is usually your hotline to your subconscious.

Do you notice any patterns and themes that stand out in your answers? How do your answers here compare to the other exercises you have completed? You are developing more of an understanding of how, when, and why you respond the way you do in certain situations. You are getting to know yourself in a deeper way.

Now look over your answers from the exercise in chapter 1 and think about what happens when you use these impulsive reactions. In your notebook, write a trigger that precedes the impulsive reaction. What are the situations or things that prompt your impulsive reaction response? Do you self-sabotage, avoid, or lash-out? For example, self-sabotaging may be connected to the trigger of feeling like someone is criticizing you. If you lash out, the trigger could be the feeling of not being heard. This is another way to determine some of your triggers.

Suppose you have identified that you shut down and pout when you don't feel heard or acknowledged. What does this remind you of from your early life? Perhaps you tried to get your mom or dad's attention and you were ignored, shut down, or discounted. Now think about how this wounded part shows up in your adult life. Does this behavior happen in your primary relationship, with friends, or with coworkers? When you are triggered in this way, do you become really quiet? How old do you feel when this happens?

Now think about what you want to say or do when this hurt gets triggered. You may either shut down or want to scream and shout and run about. Do you want to yell so that you are heard? Do you react by shouting and raging? Does this impulsive reaction match the age of wounding you identified earlier? Save your answers to use in another exercise later in the chapter.

Once I became an adult, whenever someone around me was mad, angry, out of control, or I was in a chaotic situation, my age of wounding, my little ten-year-old self who was trapped in that snow globe, was reminded of my childhood household all over again and would get scared and triggered. I would shut down, try to be perfect, and try to control my surroundings. In other words, I was doing the same things as an adult that I did as an ten-year-old boy. Once I was triggered, my little boy self would shove my adult self out of the way, step in front, and take control. This all happens unconsciously until we identify the triggers, see the patterns, and heal the lost inner child.

Take a moment now to go within and look at the ways your wounded little child inside has tried to communicate with you over the years. How has this part reacted when it was triggered after becoming afraid, scared, terrified, betrayed, or hurt? These behaviors and impulsive reactions will continue to play out until you can correlate triggers to the emotional wounding.

If you were able to identify some of your triggers with these exercises, wonderful. If not, it's OK. You will understand more about yourself and the triggers that activate your wounded inner child as we continue, and all will become clearer.

In the next section you will begin to have a dialogue and develop a connection with your wounded, lost inner child. This part of you is buried deep, but as you have learned, it still comes out to protect you when it is triggered and then goes dormant again, waiting for the next trigger.

Your next goal is to develop a connection with this part so that it is no longer isolated, cut off, and invalidated. Through this process you are learning how to characterize this wounded part of yourself so that you can develop a connection. One of the ways you can connect to this wounded part is through writing *healing letters* to yourself. But first, let's look at Judith's story.

Story: Judith, a Rejected Teenage Girl

Judith, a forty-year-old mom of a girl and a boy, had a loving family and great friends but was unhappy and critical of herself. She told me her childhood was great, that she came from a loving home, and that she had never experienced trauma or had any seriously bad things happen in her childhood. I asked her where she thought her negative self-talk and self-criticism came from, as she was not born with those messages. She said she didn't know, that "it was all good from what I remember."

Judith went to college, got married, got a job, and had kids. Meanwhile, the sense that something was wrong with her was always in the background, in her perception of herself, and in how she interacted with others. No matter how much success she had and how much her husband and kids said they loved her, she doubted herself, felt unworthy, put herself down, and wondered what others thought about her. She was critical and demanding of herself, and would never just sit down and relax. She was always overdoing in an attempt to show that she was worthy.

Judith came to see me and began the HEAL process. In our work together, I asked her to write down the wounded and the functional emotional response tools that she learned in childhood and the boundaries she set with herself and others. She then wrote out her self-talk and identified where each idea or negative belief about herself came from. She wrote out her timeline from birth to age twenty so she could see the chain of events that contributed to her sense of low self-worth and negative self-talk. This was when her age of wounding revealed itself.

Even though Judith hadn't experienced any traumatic events, some things did happen that left her deeply disappointed and affected how she felt about herself. When she was fifteen, she and her best friends tried out for the cheerleading squad, and all of the girls were picked except her. She saw this as rejection, and it deeply impacted her sense of self-worth and identity. She felt like something was wrong with her, and she became harder on herself, self-critical and judgmental.

She made up stories about why she wasn't picked and what the other girls thought about her. *Do they still like me? Why didn't Joanna call me? Has she dumped me too? What did I do wrong? What can I do to make her like me?* The rejection that Judith felt from this experience was a significant wounding that caused her to develop a deep insecurity and disconnect from her authentic self.

This initial rejection was coupled with the fact that her mother, who was a perfectionist, demanded more from Judith than she could give. Her mom would follow her around to make sure her room was showroom ready and her homework and chores were done. She yelled at her if anything was out of place or out of order. Judith began to think, *I'm stupid. I should know better. That was dumb.* Her negative self-talk established a firm footing inside and was reinforced by her mom pointing out all the things she did wrong but rarely what she did right.

While Judith had a loving home, this level of perfection was a burden. She developed insecure feelings of not being enough. She was making up stories that her friends didn't like her, and her mom reinforced these messages when Judith didn't do things perfectly. To cope with her swirling emotions, she developed the wounded emotional response tools of perfectionism, controlling behaviors, mind reading, overcompensation, and distrust.

Once she was an adult, Judith's fifteen-year-old self carried her shame wounding with her. When Judith felt left out or imagined that her friends didn't like her, this wounded part would step in front of her adult self. She spent hours each day mind reading, storytelling, and wondering, *Does she like me? Is she mad at me? Why hasn't she returned my text? Why wasn't I invited?* She would then send out texts asking, *Do you still like me? Are we good? What can I do to make this better?* Her adult self knew that this was ridiculous, that she had good friends, but she was still worried that they were going to reject her. Her age of wounding kept stepping up, frantically looking for reassurance that she was OK.

Judith's responsible adult self would eventually have to clean up the mess that her insecure fifteen-year-old self would make. She would regroup, center herself, and be an adult again. She would look back over the texts or calls that her wounded self had made, leading her to feel ashamed and juvenile for behaving that way. Shame piled on top of shame, and she didn't understand why she repeated this behavior over and over.

Through the self-exploration exercises in the HEAL process, Judith uncovered the emotional and thought patterns that she had developed in childhood and how they had set the stage for her feelings of insecurity and being less-than. She saw where her impulsive reactions and wounded emotional tools came from, and she felt ready to let them go and develop mature, functional tools.

Once she had a stronger sense of self, Judith was ready to connect to her fifteen-year-old self. After she had uncovered her age of wounding and examined how she was impacted by her mother's control, Judith wrote a series of healing letters from her younger wounded self and to that wounded part from her adult self. (You will learn shortly how to write these letters to yourself.) Through these letters, Judith finally began to hear and acknowledge her younger self and her pain.

Judith's wounded inner child outlined all of the feelings that were trapped in time. Over a series of back-and-forth letters, the emotional wounding information was being brought out, examined, held, and observed, and her wounded self began to develop a greater perspective. This younger self began to see that she wasn't flawed, that this was just an illusion based on a series of events.

Judith saw how these childhood events contributed to and supported a false sense of self, her false narrative. She saw that her mom was just being herself but also that her mom's own issues greatly contributed to Judith's insecurities, her need to control, her mistrust of herself and others, and her belief that she wasn't good enough.

Through conscious work her negative self-talk went way down, and her storytelling and mind reading also dissipated. She developed a more healed perspective of herself as time went on. She learned to use the functional emotional response tools of taking a deep breath, calming herself down, giving herself a compliment, and relaxing about the house not being showroom ready. As she did her healing work, her husband noticed that she was less angry and more relaxed. She learned to not displace her angry feelings onto her kids. She learned that her issues didn't need to become her children's burden. She still gets upset at her kids, but she has a better perspective today. She is no longer lost in her inner child wounding of playing out these old dramas from her childhood. She is learning to be kinder to herself first, and kinder to others.

Today Judith feels more freedom in her life. She feels more like herself as she is reclaiming her power. Her husband is grateful for her healing work and sees that she no longer has the nervous and insecure behaviors that she used to.

Writing Healing Letters to Yourself

Writing *healing letters* to and from yourself is a great way to immediately get feelings out and connect to that wounded part of yourself. These letters are written in a stream-of-consciousness style, that is, fast and without editing or judging. With this style of writing, you sit down and get it all out without overthinking or pre-thinking what you are going to write. That inner wounding is looking to be heard and acknowledged, and this process is a helpful and efficient way to do so. These letters are meant just for you.

The main goal in writing these letters is to connect to the frozen part of you that carries the wounding. Once you form this connection you will begin to see, hear, and feel how your wounding shows up in your adult life. The letters will create a bridge that will bring your frozen wounding into the light of day.

The process sounds simple, and it is, yet it does many things all at once and works on many levels. After you have written the first letters, you will be able to connect to your feelings in a different way than when you just think about or express the thoughts verbally. You will be giving yourself permission to fully and freely express emotions that have been bottled up or unexpressed for a long time. Letter writing provides a safe outlet for this contained and bottled-up energy.

Putting pen to paper accesses a deep part of us. The kinetic movement forms a bridge between the conscious and the subconscious. When we use our fine motor skills to write out our feelings, we are giving the heart a pathway to release pent-up emotion.

Once we put our thoughts and feelings onto paper, we can face them and learn how to hold them in a new way. This takes tremendous courage, which is why people will put off doing this simple exercise. However, you have come this far in the process and can no longer deny that events happened in childhood that affect you as an adult.

Please remember that these letters are a form of focused writing. They are not meant for anyone other than you. Please keep them for now, as you will look back over them when you get to chapter 8.

With humility, I surrender to my own feelings.

Letter from Your Younger Self to Your Adult Self

The first letter you write will be from a younger wounded part of you to your adult self. The goal of this letter writing exchange is to bring into the light of day the pain, confusion, misunderstanding, distortion, and false narrative that the younger self carries. After all, it is this lack of perspective that keeps the younger self stuck and always on guard. This letter exchange is designed to clearly state what those issues are and spell out how they got that way. The responsible adult self then has the opportunity to respond, clear up misconceptions, and give the younger self the love, validation, trust, and respect that it has never have had before.

I have found that it is more effective to have the inner child write the first letter because this is where the pain is held, and the inner child will reveal the emotional woundings for the adult self to address in the return letter.

Before you write your first letter, it may be helpful to read a sample letter. The following is a letter from my little boy self to my adult self.

> *Dear adult me,*
>
> *I'm ten years old, and I am feeling overwhelmed and sad. Mother and Dad keep fighting every night it seems, and I don't know what to do. I'm really feeling lost. I'm tired, scared, and my tummy hurts. I've tried to be good and even perfect, but that didn't help. I feel like giving up or running away because I don't know what to do with everything I feel.*
>
> *I watch to see what their moods are like and try not to do or say anything that will upset them. But it's confusing because sometimes they are loving and fun, but other times they are upset with each other and yell at me. Sometimes I want to scream at all of this, and other times I want to be invisible.*
>
> *It doesn't make sense to me, and I just go in my room and cry into my pillow because I don't want anyone to see me. I just want to go away and hide from this. It's just too much. I don't know what to do, and I feel hurt and lonely now, and I feel all alone, and I feel like no one is going to ever love me. I don't feel lovable because I'm doing something wrong and they are upset. I am sad and angry.*

As I wrote this letter from my little boy self, tears were flowing and I was flushed with sadness, frustration, anger, and rage. I was barely able to read my writing because I had scrawled across the page so fast and furiously.

Through writing these letters, I gave my younger self a voice. I could see, hear, and feel the deep anguish that I carried all those years. I was connecting the dots and seeing how my younger wounded parts were showing up in my adult life by my attempts to control others, feeling less-than and lonely, and letting my anger come out passive-aggressively.

By writing these feelings out, I began to feel a shift and a release. I was learning to describe those feelings from long ago, and I felt grateful that I could get them out of me. I was acknowledging all of those feelings that had been trapped, and in doing so, I could stop using the impulsive reactions that were negatively impacting my adult life.

Do not overthink what you will write before you start writing. This is an immersive, reflexive experience, where you let the words flow naturally. Your inner child has a lot to say, so you will not need to script it. The younger self will state its clear emotions, which will become the road map for the letter from your adult self in response.

To write this first letter from your younger self, you need to get inside your own head and heart at the age of wounding. In other words, start to remember what was happening at that age, where you were living, who was there, what the mood was, and most importantly, what you were feeling. Connecting with some emotional pain here is a key part of this process. If you keep these letters on a superficial level, you will not get the results you desire. Give yourself permission to pull up the hurt, pain, anger, sadness, and frustration that lives inside you and in this wounded part.

Putting pen to paper establishes a deep connection with your subconscious emotional memory. There is something about forming the letters, words, and sentences with pen in hand that unlocks emotional memories buried deep inside as you describe the pain. Your younger self may be skeptical of this first attempt, so don't think that there is going to be a tremendous breakthrough all at once. The first letter will set the stage and prepare you to go deeper with subsequent letters.

YOUR TURN

Find a quiet place to do this work. If you can't find a quiet place at home, be creative. Is there a secluded place or backyard you can sit in for privacy? Before you start writing, read through the instructions so you won't have to stop in the middle of writing.

Start with a blank sheet of paper. Look over your timeline, and identify the specific age of wounding and the event that you are ready to write about. Close your eyes and begin to ask that wounded part to describe how they feel. Begin to connect with your wounded and lost inner child. The following questions can help you visualize the setting.

- How old is this part of you?
- What was going on in the household?
- Who was there?
- What did it feel, sound, and smell like?
- What was happening?
- What you were feeling?
- What are the secrets this part has been holding on to?
- What are the deep, heavy hurts this part carries?
- What does your child self want to say to your responsible adult self?

When you are ready, start writing. Don't think about it, just write. Keep pushing your pen or pencil to move, and let out whatever comes. It doesn't have to make sense, and you don't even have to be able to read it. Write fast and furiously; don't edit or worry about good penmanship. Be in the flow of the moment. (Sometimes people ask if they can type their letter, and certainly that works, but there is a difference between the two modalities. Try both ways to see which one gives you deeper results.)

Transfer your feelings and thoughts onto the paper. Write for as long as it takes. Don't stop until you feel you have said what you wanted to say. If there is more inside of you, keep going until you can't think of another thing your wounded part wants or needs to say.

Don't rush through the exercise or think you have to quickly move ahead to the next part of the process. Be gentle with yourself right now; pushing yourself through the work is not going to heal you faster.

Letter writing will help you begin to understand what this wounded part feels and sounds like, and to identify when it shows up in your adult life. Once you can recognize what your wounded part does and says and what triggers it, then you can address your impulsive reactions in real time.

If you find writing from the perspective of your younger self difficult, try describing the wounding events from your childhood by symbolically writing to a friend or an anonymous person. The key is to connect with the emotions related to the situation, as this is going to help in the next step, when your adult self writes back.

Letter from Your Adult Self to Your Younger Self

Now you are ready for your adult self to connect with your younger self. Ideally your adult self will be loving, caring, and nurturing. After all, you just heard your younger self reveal all the painful emotions that it has been holding on to for so many years.

As you already know, your responsible adult self is the part of you that has matured, pays the bills, and does the work of being an adult in the world. It is your grounded part. Your younger self needs to hear from your protective, responsible adult self that you will set strong boundaries, and that you can handle whatever it was that created the woundings and triggers in the first place. If the younger self doesn't believe you, or if you do not create strong boundaries, then the younger self will not put down its wounded emotional response tools.

As before, it can help to see an example of this letter writing. The following is the response from my adult self to my younger self.

Dear little Bobby,

I love you so much, and I'm so proud of how hard you have worked to try to make things better for Mother, Dad, and your sister. I know that things are really confusing for you right now. As much as I know you want to fix everything and make it all better and be perfect, that's not your job. Your job is to be a ten-year-old boy and a big brother to your sister, to go out and play with your friends, do your chores, and feel your freedom. Mother and Dad and the entire family love you more than you know, and more than they are able to express at times.

When you feel lost, tired, and sad, know that I see you as perfect, whole, and complete. Even though you feel lost, you are part of a big, loving family that is sometimes kinda wacky, but there is a lot of love there.

I want you to know that Dad yells at you from his pain and fear. He doesn't know how to express his feelings in a good way, and then when he drinks too much, he gets loud and scary. Just know that he loves you, and when you get older, you are going to be able to appreciate and receive his love and respect him for the man he is.

I know you cry yourself to sleep at night and have tummy aches from the stress of it all, and that you feel sad and confused most days. You will eventually be able to express your feelings and be heard, and to feel that you are worthy. You will begin to trust yourself and your feelings so that you don't have to be perfect to be loved and to make it all better for everyone else.

Mother's going to be fine. I know you try to help her when she looks sad or worried. I know you think about how she is doing and what you can do to make things better. It may be hard to understand now, but Mother is trying hard, just like you, to make things better. You are learning from her how to be kind, loving, and compassionate, and how to smooth things over when Dad or others are upset.

I want you to know and to feel in your heart that I am here for you. I am learning how to set boundaries to protect you and me as the adult. You don't need to work so hard at protecting me, you don't have to be perfect, you don't have to make others feel better, and you don't have to smooth things out for everyone else. Let me protect you like the older brother you always wanted to have watch out for you. You are not alone.

I love you.

Adult me

Take a deep breath. What was it like for you to read this letter? What feelings came up? Pay attention to those feelings, as they are clues to help you know more about yourself and your woundings.

You can see the consistent messages of love in my letter to little Bobby. My responsible adult self reassures him that my boundary setting is strong and that it is OK to have feelings. When you write your letters, you can write about the events that were happening to establish a context, but focus on the emotions you felt at the time. The wounded child self needs to have emotional validation in order to begin the healing process. In doing so, your inner child will begin to trust you, to know that you will be there and that you won't abandon this part. Resist the urge to admonish, criticize, or tell the wounded inner child what it should be doing or what needs to be done to fix everything. This part already worked overtime to try and make this out-of-control situation better. What it needs now is acknowledgment, love, kindness, and validation.

Before we move on to the next letter writing, here is another sample letter from the adult self to the child self that a patient of mine gave permission to share.

Dear Becky,

For some reason you never believed that you were good enough or pretty enough or smart enough. I'm here to tell you that is not true. There are all sorts of reasons why you felt that way: being adopted, looking different, having parents that didn't fit in and a brother who was unpopular and had troubles of his own, and having friends who didn't know how to be good friends. I see your struggles, sadness, and loneliness, and that's OK. I know that you are going to grow up and, with some help, feel better about yourself.

I know your friends don't always treat you well. I know this is confusing and that you sometimes think something is wrong with you. But this is not who you are.

All of what you experienced shaped who you were and who I am today. These experiences made me look at who I am and who I want to be. Even though I spent years ignoring your feelings and pushing them down, I assure you that I will now be able to become closer to the person I want to be for myself, my family, my children, my community, and my world.

I see how hard you work and how much you want to please others. As a grown-up, I am learning to take care of the adult me through my words and actions. In turn, this will help you feel safer and stronger. You are learning, evolving, and growing. I made this affirmation for us:

I trust the evolution of my life, and I am exactly where I am supposed to be.

Love,

Me

Becky's letter connects with the wounded inner child self that still spins in the dysfunctional feelings and illusions of her youth. Her adult self is reaching through time and extending herself emotionally to connect with this wounded part. She addresses some of the struggles from that time and emphasizes what is happening emotionally.

Becky's wounded part shows up in her adult life through low self-esteem, emotionally shutting down, avoiding confrontation, and feeling lonely and isolated. The letter is her invitation to her younger self to let go of some of this wounding because her adult self is learning how to take care of and set boundaries for herself. She is trying to give perspective to the emotions and the situation.

When you write your first adult letter, you may not know where to begin. If this is the case, start by describing the situation your younger self wrote about in the first letter. Use the same feeling words your younger self used. The language you use with your younger self is all about emotional validation and acknowledgment.

Once you know the type of the language to use and what you want to acknowledge, you are ready to write to your younger self. Explain that you know the situation and that it was painful. You know the hurts and sorrows and that this younger part was betrayed, for example.

You may remember how you wished that someone older could have explained things to you. This is what you will be doing as you write this letter to your younger self.

Before you start writing, keep in mind the key elements that the wounded part needs to know, hear, and feel from your adult self:

- Acknowledge all of the pain and wounding that this part carries, and validate specific feelings from that time.
- Let this part know that you will not abandon or ignore it until it is healed and integrated with your adult self.
- State that you will protect all parts of your wounded inner child by establishing strong boundaries for yourself and others.

Your Turn

As before, find a quiet place to do this letter writing. Sit quietly for a minute or two, and take a few deep, relaxing breaths. Start with a blank sheet of paper. Begin the letter with "Dear little ..." Tell your inner child what you know it is yearning to hear. Tell this part that it is being cared for.

Your inner child may need to hear a lot of reassurance from you, especially if you grew up in a highly dysregulated household or experienced multiple betrayals or severe traumas. If this is the case, your inner child is pretty well guarded. This part has learned to protect itself and may not trust you even as you say that everything will be OK. Be patient, as this wounding has been there for years, and it is going to take a while to process the hurts.

Above all, don't stop and shut down. You are at a crucial part of your journey of healing. Don't leave your younger self hanging out there after it bared its soul. Write from a place of loving kindness, understanding, and compassion for this wise part of you.

Writing these letters is tough work. After you have written your letters, go out and take a walk, connect with nature, and drink lots of water. These actions are great grounding exercises and will help you to feel more solid within yourself, especially after you have processed deep emotional pain.

Moving through the Process

Once you have written a few letters back and forth with your younger self, ask yourself if this wounded part of you is shifting inside. Is it evolving or transforming? Are things moving around a bit so that you are beginning to have a different perspective? Does the event still feel as intense as it once did? Are emotions easing up, or are they staying the same? Review your timeline and your Emotional Response Scale ratings. Are the ratings still the same, or have they decreased?

If the letters are not creating any shifts inside, you may need to dig deeper and be more heartfelt with the writing. If you are keeping it all on a surface level and not going deep within yourself to find the pain, you will not have much movement from this exercise. If you feel resistant to going deeper, then look at that issue. Do you not want to feel the pain again? Are you afraid that if you heal the pain, you won't know what your life will be like in the future? Be gentle with yourself. Observe, don't condemn, yourself.

One challenge you may have is that you are still learning how to set boundaries and are not good at it yet, so you are not sure how to reassure the wounded part. That's OK. The biggest thing I find is that the wounded part just wants to be heard and validated. You may need to fake it before you make it with boundary setting, but as long as you are moving forward with the letter exchange and are strong and loving with yourself, you are making progress.

Another challenge is that you may still feel the same way you did as a child, so you don't feel that you can write your adult letter yet because the pain you feel as an adult mirrors how you felt as a child.

Or you may wonder how you can reassure your child self when you don't know if things are going to be OK. Just remember that you do know how your life story turns out so far because you are here reading this book and doing this work.

Your life may not be perfect, but whatever was happening in your childhood has ceased. You have the battle scars from that time, but those harmful experiences are no longer happening. If you are unsure of what words to use, I recommend that you write the adult letters in the words and intentions of a respectful, loving, and kind teacher or coach you knew growing up. Pick up on this strong, loving energy and then put into words what the wounded part needs to hear.

Every child wants to hear that things are going to be OK. The adult may not always know if things really are going to be OK, but the adult carries that hopeful strength for the child. The adult can shoulder the responsibility for saying things are going to be OK because the adult is going to do everything they can to make it OK for the child. It is their highest intention.

Again, be gentle with yourself. The process of opening up pathways inside that you have not uncovered for years is magical. It is a journey into a familiar place that has been in the dark for a long time. There is a wellspring of emotion that reveals itself in this expression, but you have to give yourself permission to be vulnerable to touch this treasure.

Story: Letters from Jason, a Teenage Boy

Jason is a forty-three-year-old married man with children. He came to see me because he was not fulfilled in his marriage.

He and his wife have no emotionally intimacy. He avoids discussions, and at times lies to her to get out of any conflict.

Jason has given permission for me to share his healing letters. The following is a back-and-forth exchange between his fourteen-year-old wounded self and his responsible adult self. The first is from his younger self.

Hello Older Me,

Oh, man, a lot of things have happened lately. One of my best friends died in a car accident. His older brother was driving drunk. They sideswiped another car, veered off the road, and crashed head on into a tree. Killed my friend and another person in the car. I don't even know what to say. I feel shell-shocked, like this isn't real. But he's gone, and now there's a hole in me.

We hung out almost every day. We had talked about making a band. He even got drums and found a beat-up acoustic guitar and gave it to me. Now the band will never happen.

My family seems to understand what's going on with me and has given me space, but we never talk about it. I guess they don't know what to say. I feel like they just look at me and wonder what I'm going to do.

I still have my other best friend and friends I hang out with. We mostly sit around and drink and smoke and do whatever. Because of all this, and because I wasn't listening to Mom and her rules, she made me move in with Dad. This means I can't go to high school with my friends.

I'm going to this new school where everyone knows each other but me. I walk through the hallways like I'm a ghost. I look around and see people having a good time, the guys talking to girls and stuff. I talk to a few people, and I act like this tough guy, like I have it all together. But I feel so alone and scared all the time, and it makes me angry that I have to go through this. Every chance I get, I go hang out with my friends from before. At least I still get to do that, sometimes.

Living with Dad has its ups and downs. It feels good to finally get to be around him a lot. It feels like he does care now, and we do have some good times, but I still feel angry and sad and lonely a lot.

I still close myself off in my room and zone out in my world of pity. Sometimes it gets so bad that I cry myself to sleep at night, wishing I could be someone else. I don't know why I feel like something is wrong with me so strongly, but it hurts. I feel like nobody understands, and there's nothing I can do. Seems like I'm supposed to go on with life like everything is fine. All I can do is try to be alone or go hang with my friends and drink or smoke pot or do things that would get me in trouble if I got caught. Does life get better? Will I ever feel OK?

In Jason's adult response, notice how loving and supportive he is toward his younger part.

Dear Fourteen-Year-Old Me,

You lost someone who was very important to you, and that's so hard to go through, especially when it doesn't seem like there's anyone who can help.

Your family loves you very much and are doing their best. You just do whatever you need to feel that sadness as much as you need to. There's no need to hide it or pretend you're OK. Throw in starting at a new school and not knowing anybody, and whoa, what a crazy, rough thing to go through.

Give yourself credit for not completely losing it. Give yourself credit for having the courage to do what you need to do.

Please know that even though your family doesn't know what to say or do to make things better for you, they love you very much. You know deep down that you are a good person. You just need to believe that you are worthy of love and good things in your life.

Love,

Adult me

I feel fortunate that Jason allowed me to share his letter exchange with you. His letters demonstrate his heartfelt nature and his intimate connection with the pain his younger self carried. In his letter to his fourteen-year-old self, you can hear the language of an older brother or mentor. He is kind and clear with his words and perspectives. He also reassures his younger self by saying, *I see you, I hear you, and I know you're going to be OK.* He encourages his younger part that he doesn't need to stay stuck, that he can feel his feelings, let go of some of the pain, and mature emotionally.

Jason went on to write more back-and-forth letters to help his wounded inner child heal and to stop some behaviors he was doing in his adult life that were rooted in his adolescent wounding. His younger part showed up in his adult life by lying, avoiding, being passive-aggressive, and wanting covert control. He had tried other types of therapies, but none of them got to the root of the issue. His goal now is to bring forth the wounding so he can heal it with the adult self's grounded emotional maturity.

You could probably feel the pain and sincerity in Jason's letters, which set the path for his younger self to heal. Making this sort of connection with your younger self will create emotional shifts inside of you, too. That is the difference between writing a letter just to do the exercise and writing a letter to bring about lasting change within yourself.

You may be wondering how many times you need to do this back-and-forth letter writing. Most people do so four or five times. I find that this number of exchanges is effective in helping to process many of the feelings that the younger self holds and the adult self needs to address. Your letters may be many pages or just one page, but I do encourage you to write more than just a few sentences.

If you don't feel any emotion and just state the facts as you write your letters, you need to get out of your head and spend more time sitting and accessing your emotions. Stick with it. (Refer to the Feelings Chart in appendix A if you are stuck for words and need some prompting.) Your younger wounded self has a lot to say to you. When the younger self doesn't have any further urge to express the pain through letters, you will have released everything that has been pressing up against the doorway, and you will feel the shift within.

How do you feel now that you have written your letters? Over the next few days, notice how your younger self shows up in your adult life. Just live your life, and see if you can make some connections between the emotions you felt during the events on your timeline and the emotions you feel now. Learn to listen for this younger part of you. Notice the words you use to tell people how you feel.

Notice how you may be pausing for a moment before you respond to a situation. Notice when you are not quite feeling yourself; this indicates that a shift is occurring. Take a moment to acknowledge that you used to react a certain way to your triggers but can now choose how to respond. You can determine whether the younger self is stepping in front or your adult self is taking charge, setting boundaries, and reassuring the younger wounded self that everything is going to be OK. Remember, the younger self is not going to put down the impulsive response tools until the adult self becomes the one in charge and is protective of all the parts.

Assess Your Progress

You have done a lot of deep healing work so far. Let's take a moment to take inventory, assess your progress, and see how you are doing.

You are looking at yourself in new ways as you determine when and how this younger wounded self starts to step in front of you. You are looking over your letters and hearing what the younger part is saying. You are seeing where this part is getting stuck. You are hearing what this part is looking for, yearning for, and desperate for. The more you address these core emotional needs, the more the younger self is going to start to heal and integrate with the adult self, which is the final goal of the HEAL process. Pay attention to what the younger self says and how it communicates.

You may now see that this wounded part is sad, lonely, childish with words, or even a brat. You may see how this part demonstrates itself with throwing tantrums or withholding or controlling. In whatever way your wounding comes out, remember that this is just how it is trying to get your attention. It is not good or bad. Give yourself permission to just observe this and hold it, knowing you are working on transforming this emotional energy inside of you.

EXERCISE: DEVELOPING FUNCTIONAL TOOLS TO MANAGE TRIGGERING EVENTS

This exercise will help you to identify more clearly where each trigger came from, what it needs in order to heal, and how to make a plan for using functional tools.

Take out your notebook and review the list of triggers you wrote down in "Exercise: Identify Your Triggers" earlier in this chapter. Next to each trigger, write down where that trigger came from and what it needs in order to heal. For example:

> Trigger: Being disrespected. This trigger really bothers me. It comes from never feeling heard or valued. This part needs to be honored and heard, and I need to set stronger boundaries with people.

Once you have identified the source of a trigger, come up with a plan for your responsible adult self to remain in charge. For example, you can make an agreement with the younger wounded part that you are going to be proactive and take care of all of this wounding now that you have a good idea of where your triggers come from, what they are, what your impulsive reactions are to your triggers, and what you want to do to HEAL this cycle. You are building a set of functional response tools to add to your toolbox.

This trigger list and your functional response toolbox will help your adult self remember what you need to do to take care of yourself emotionally every day. The more you consciously work on developing new functional tools and addressing your triggers each day, the sooner you will shift out of the dysfunctional dance with your wounding. This is a daily practice that you will need to remind yourself to do at first, but once you get in the habit, it will feel natural.

The emotional shifts you are making at this time are big, but there will still be times when the shadows of your emotional pain or wounding show up. For example, you may yell, act impulsively, throw tantrums, or be moody. That's fine. It means that the wounded part is still getting triggered. This work is not about being perfect, it is about acknowledging and discerning what is working for you and what is not.

After you have responded to a person or situation, ask yourself if the response was the best grounded response you could have given at the time. Look below the surface of the pain, disappointment, and hurt to determine the root of these behavioral choices. If emotions and impulsive reactions keep resurfacing, you may need to do more letter writing to understand the origins of the wounding better. Be patient and stick with it.

As you progress along in the HEAL process, you may find that after you have addressed the needs of one wounded part of you, another one bubbles up to the surface, and along with it a second age of wounding saying, *Now it's my turn.*

If other areas of wounding start coming forward, go through the letter writing process again with these new wounded feelings. Notice the language that your younger self uses to express the feelings and experiences from that time, then take your time responding in the same gentle way you did before.

You may also have an issue resurface that you thought you had already dealt with, or you may feel like you are going backward when these old patterns and feelings show up. This is just the shadow of old emotional programming presenting itself at a different time in your life. It is showing up again because you need to examine a different part of this dynamic. It is not good or bad, it is just a natural part of the healing progression. If this happens, repeat the HEAL process you have done so far, and address this shadow.

You have explored a lot about yourself in this chapter by creating your timeline, rating the intensity of your experiences, determining your age of wounding, understanding your triggers, and writing healing letters back and forth with your younger self. If you completed all of the exercises and processes in this chapter, congratulations! That is tremendous work. If you shied away from some of them, that's OK, too. This resistance is just fear of the unknown. Keep on your path, and do the work as you are able to. All is in the right time and order.

You are well on your way to healing the woundings that you suffered during childhood. You know much more about yourself now than you ever have, and you are setting yourself up for living an authentic life. In the next chapter you will begin the work of learning to set healthy boundaries, a major key in healing your lost inner child.

CHAPTER 6

Boundaries

Love yourself more than you love your drama.

—JEN SINCERO, *YOU ARE A BADASS*

One of the most important steps you will take as you work through the HEAL process is to learn how to set healthy boundaries. The goal of the work in this chapter is for you to be able to clearly determine your boundary status with yourself and others. Through the exercises in the chapter, you will determine your boundary status by evaluating where you practice healthy functional boundaries and where you have broken boundaries.

Healthy boundary setting is a big key to making the HEAL process work. Establishing functional boundaries creates an environment for the healing to happen and sets the stage to integrate the frozen, wounded younger self with the responsible adult self. Boundaries form the bridge for the wounded self to grow up emotionally and discard the wounded defensiveness. Once healthy boundaries are established, the wounded part can set down the wounded emotional response tools and impulsive reactions, and integrate with the responsible adult self.

Boundaries help you to discern who and what you are, who you are not, what you want, and what you don't want. Through boundary setting, you will develop the skill of discernment and find those aspects of yourself that are in alignment, matching who you are. You will also be able to recognize unhealthy, fuzzy, or nonexistent boundaries so that you can see where healing is needed.

An elaborate dance happens when you are developing a connection to your younger wounded self: the younger self is looking to see if the responsible adult self can be trusted. The wounded part really wants to trust the responsible adult self, but the reality is that the younger self has had to take charge in triggering situations for decades. It will keep using the wounded emotional tools until a sense of trust and connection is made. This is what you were doing with the letter writing exercise in the last chapter. You were forming trust and connection with your wounded part so that the handover and integration could happen and the wounded part could learn to trust your adult self.

The responsible adult self needs to be consistent and show that clear boundaries can and must be set with people who are abusive, mean, or otherwise triggering to the wounded part. At the same time, the adult self needs to be clear with internal boundaries and what is healthy and productive in thinking, feeling, and being.

Creating Healthy Boundaries

Boundaries are about being able to say no to others as a way to protect yourself physically, emotionally, mentally, and sexually, and knowing what is good for you and what is not. Whatever boundary system your parents had when you were growing up, chances are you use similar boundaries as an adult. You watched how your parents responded to situations, if they gave in and didn't hold their boundaries, or if they put up walls and shut out others—including you—and you picked up on all of them. You took in all of these boundary responses and thought that was how you should handle such situations.

Healthy boundaries are about having clarity around how we feel. The more we set healthy boundaries, the more clarity we have, and the more clarity we have, the more all parts of us feel connected, safe, and authentic. We feel free and fully integrated with the true self when we set boundaries.

You must let go of the outcome when you set a boundary. For example, when you say, "No, I don't want to go out tonight," you are not attaching any strings or manipulating the other person; you are simply expressing your feelings out loud. Boundary statements are not about being unfeeling or uncaring, as that would be shutting down your feelings or closing yourself off from others in an unhealthy way. They are about being fully connected to all parts of yourself. From this centered place you can determine how you feel about a situation, event, or comment and then decide how you want to act based on those feelings.

Strong boundaries mean we honor ourselves (internal boundaries) and stand up for ourselves (external boundaries).

In her book *Facing Codependence: What It Is, Where It Comes From, How It Sabotages Our Lives*, international authority on codependence Pia Mellody goes into great detail about external and internal boundaries and how they are shaped by our childhood family. She describes boundary systems as "invisible and symbolic 'force fields' that have three purposes: (1) to keep people from coming into our space and abusing us, (2) to keep us from going into the space of others and abusing them, and (3) to give each of us a way to embody our sense of 'who we are.'"[1]

Let's look more deeply at internal and external boundaries and how to set them.

Setting Internal Boundaries

Internal boundaries are personal statements or agreements that you have with yourself regarding a particular issue. You make these silent statements regarding multiple issues throughout each day. Internal boundaries are not necessarily discussed with others, as they are internal contracts with yourself. Internal boundaries help you be responsible to and for yourself.

The following are examples of *internal boundary* statements:

- I am not going to go to the bar with my friends because I know that environment is not good for me.
- I am not going to yell, scream, demand, deceive, blame, ridicule, or demean others.
- I am not going to take in the criticisms of others.
- I am going to be honest and vulnerable with myself.
- I am going to honor myself today and not beat up on myself if I make a mistake.
- I am going to keep my commitment to myself and go to the gym at least twice a week.
- I am going to find a therapist to help me with my depression and anxiety.

---

1. Pia Mellody, *Facing Codependence: What It Is, Where It Comes From, How It Sabotages Our Lives*, HarperCollins, New York, 2003.

- I am going to maintain strong boundaries with others and say no when I need to.
- I am going to keep a gratitude journal of all the things that I am grateful for each day.
- I am going to smile more and practice finding the good in myself and others.

These are examples of making commitments to oneself and how to honor and respect those commitments. People who know themselves have a strong internal boundary system. People who look to others to define their world often have fuzzy internal boundaries and are all over the place when it comes to decision making. They give others the power to define their internal reality and identity.

Setting External Boundaries

External boundaries are statements or positions you establish with another person or situation. External boundaries are in place when you have clarity internally about what you want or don't want and then express this clarity to another person in simple, clear, and assertive statements. External boundaries often begin with an "I" statement. For example:

- I feel hurt that you didn't include me.
- I feel that my personal space is being disrespected. I don't like it when you stand so close to me. Can you step back?
- I feel confused about why you don't ask me for help.
- I feel hurt because of the way you continually talk down to me.
- I feel trusting and safe in our relationship.
- I feel excited that you are taking me on the trip with you.

- I feel great gratitude and joy that you are my friend. Thank you for being in my life.
- I am going to respect you and your personal property by not snooping or listening in, and I ask for the same from you (internal and external boundaries).
- I feel uncomfortable doing what you want me to do sexually.
- I will be respectful of you and will try not to control you.
- I will respect you when you say no, and I ask you to respect me when I say no.

Internal and external boundary statements are not always about saying no. They can also state what you will do or agree to.

A strong boundary sense helps us
feel capable and wise.

"I" STATEMENTS

When you are making a boundary statement, it is important to make it an "I" statement. Boundary statements are not about blaming or shaming someone else, as in, "You made me angry. You are always doing this, and you never do that." The "I" statement is designed to help the other person be less defensive and thus able to hear your feelings.

To set a healthy boundary, check in with yourself in the moment and ask, *How do I feel about this person, place, or situation right now?* Your boundary statement is your gut reaction. You will have a physical reaction somewhere in your body if this idea feels good to you or not. Be careful not to override this reaction and start making excuses for the other person's behavior.

If you make up stories, this is your wounding showing up and saying you shouldn't set a boundary. *Well, he has had a hard time of it. I'll go ahead and do this for him,* or, *I don't always want to say no to her because if I do, she's not going to like me.* Most people who struggle with saying no to others do so because they don't want to offend, don't want to get into it, or are people pleasers and conflict avoiders. People who have the hardest time learning to set boundaries are those who talk themselves out of the boundary in the first place. The rule to remember is, if you don't want to do something, if you don't like something, if you don't need something, then say no. Use your discernment to figure out how you want to set your boundary.

It is harder to set boundaries in relationships that have meaning to us. We have more invested in these relationships and more to lose. Trust yourself and the relationship to hold your boundary. Any relationship worth having and developing is going to have a healthy boundary exchange. Someone who doesn't respect your boundaries usually will not have a good boundary system themselves, and chances are they are narcissistically inclined.

In professional settings we often have better boundaries because there are defined rules and we clearly know what is our work to do and what is someone else's. Most people have a good boundary sense at work, but when they get home it is as if all of this goes away. When I ask, most people will say, *yes I can set boundaries at work, but not at home,* so they are aware of their boundary skills. But in their intimate relationships they don't want to seem controlling, pushy, or mean. Functional boundary setting is not any of those things.

Boundary violations occur when our boundaries are not honored or respected. We can also violate or go against our own boundary by ignoring or pushing aside how we feel or what we mean to say.

Strong boundaries help us to stop the cycles that keep tearing down our sense of self.

The following is a story of a good man who lost his internal boundary compass.

Story: Bernard, a Married Man Having Emotional Affairs

Bernard is a successful forty-seven-year-old married father who was having emotional affairs with women. He didn't know why he was doing this, and he wanted to stop. There was a part of him that loved the excitement and adventure, but afterward, he would go into a shame spiral, regret the affair, and feel guilty when he was with his wife and family. His wife was unaware of his infidelity. He loved her, but they were not close emotionally.

When Bernard looked over the themes and patterns of his timeline, and he began to see all the areas of his childhood abandonment. His dad left his mom when Bernard was eight years old, which created a huge emotional black hole in him. For most of his life since that time he had felt empty and emotionally bankrupt. He had tried his best to create a full life for himself; he married and had a family, but inside he still felt empty.

As Bernard worked through the HEAL process, he realized that his eight-year-old wounded little boy self wanted his parents' acceptance, love, nurturing, and wholeness, and he was unconsciously trying to get that in his adult life. He began to see that one of the main reasons he kept going outside of his relationship was to feel acceptance and love, and fill up this hole.

Bernard felt this sense from his wife after they were married, and he was elated. His wife gave him what he had been searching for his entire life. However, after the kids were born, she gave all of her emotional attention to the kids, and there wasn't any left over for him. He knew she loved him, but he felt pushed aside, much like how he felt as a child. That was when his wounded little boy self began to feel the same sad, lonely, and isolated feelings again.

He would start seeking attention from other women. It always started innocently enough, with mutual interest and then flirting. It soon progressed to texting and then sexting. Bernard did not consciously realize that he was falling down this rabbit hole, and each time it was hard for him to get out.

In his sessions with me, he at first said that all he was doing was sexting, not having sex. We talked about how he was rationalizing and minimizing his actions. I asked him if he would show his wife what he was doing if she were sitting next to him while he was sexting. "Well, of course not," he said. I explained that if he wouldn't want his wife to see or know of his activity, and even if he was not having sex, he was committing an infidelity to his relationship commitment. At a deep level he was going against something that he treasured—his wife and family—just to satisfy the emotional needs of his lost inner child.

Bernard began to see how he was creating elaborate secret ways of getting love and attention from others, rationalizing his behavior and not generating any self-love on his own. He was dependent on this outside love and would always need a new supply. He was using the emotional reasoning and denial of a little boy who felt emotionally abandoned, the consequences of which his adult self had to clean up.

Bernard used the letter writing exercise to give his eight-year-old wounded little boy a voice. As he wrote multiple letters back and forth, he began to clearly see what he had emotionally needed for all of those years. He learned that he had become dependent on love and attention from outside of himself because of his initial wounding. He saw how he had created a secret life apart from his wife to get his emotional needs met. In fact, he even saw how he was getting back at his wife because she was giving love to the kids and not him. (That is an eight-year-old's emotional response.) He realized how he was keeping himself stuck in his wounding by giving in to his little boy's emotional needs each time instead of healing the core wounding.

Bernard learned how his wounded little boy was stepping in front of him and making choices that could ruin his marriage. This realization shocked him into wanting to heal this old wounding. He saw how much power he had turned over to his eight-year-old self and how this younger self was using the emotional reasoning of a child. Once he could see the whole infidelity picture, he no longer tried to rationalize or minimize it; he owned it for what it was.

Bernard began to set internal boundaries with behaviors that were good for him to do, such as loving self-care, and setting clear boundaries against behaviors that were not helping, such as talking with other women without his wife's knowledge. He made a commitment to delete the apps on his phone that he used to meet women and to end his texting/sexting relationships.

Through the HEAL process, Bernard could see how and when his younger wounded part got triggered, and he developed a plan to cope with the triggers. When his wounded self became triggered, he would stop what he was doing, acknowledge the feeling, and say loving and kind words to himself. *I am loved every day by my family and my friends. I am worth loving.* He was learning how to nurture himself with affirming messages of love.

Bernard now understood his emotional needs. He made the choice to not tell his wife about his emotional infidelities, but he did start to verbalize his feelings of loneliness and isolation to her. She had no idea that he felt that way. She felt bad because she loved him and didn't want him to suffer. She hadn't realized how much attention she had been giving to the kids and how he was feeling.

Bernard made it clear to his wife that he appreciated everything she did for the kids, for him, and for their life together. He didn't want her to think he was blaming her for his feelings or that she had done something wrong by giving love to their children. They worked on their communication, which was easier for him to do now that he had learned how to access and describe his emotions. Since he was learning to give himself the love he needed, he was not as emotionally dependent on his wife or others as he once was. He was one of the lucky ones in that he worked on these issues before his emotional acting-out destroyed his marriage.

As a side note, in my research over the years, I found that therapists are split on their opinions as to whether a person should tell their partner about an affair or not. One could ask, if he doesn't, is he adding to his secret shame and could potentially do it again? That is a valid question. Professionally, I follow the patient's agenda. In Bernard's case, it was his choice to not disclose his affairs to his wife. I saw the depth of his self-discovery and the healing that he was doing, which was fundamentally transforming his emotional landscape.

Bernard was healing from the inside out. His functional adult self could see and feel the pain and shame that his actions had caused him, and how this had spilled over into his relationship with his wife. Instead of being buried by these feelings, his responsible adult self was able to use them to establish better boundaries with himself and with his wife. He was healing and transforming this shame instead of letting it fester and become toxic. He transformed what had been a vicious cycle of self-destructive behavior by finding and using his own resilience to give to himself that which he most desired. He had always had the power within himself; the HEAL process just brought it to the surface.

Bernard made a commitment to do everything in his power to heal this part of him so he wouldn't get back on that treadmill. He told his wife his feelings and how much he loved her. He now expresses his needs and honors his commitment to his marriage. He has chosen to become integrated with his adult self and to live authentically.

SETTING RESPONSIBLE BOUNDARIES

Your goal throughout this process is to heal your inner child woundings, integrate the lost inner child with your adult self, and embrace an authentic life. Setting responsible boundaries is as important to this outcome as connecting with your emotions and your younger self. Having good boundaries will help you feel safe within yourself and in your relationships.

As a result of all the work you did in chapter 5—creating your timeline, identifying your triggers, and writing your healing letters— your wounded part is beginning to join with your responsible adult self. Your adult self is now learning to find your boundary voice for a feeling of strength, protection, purpose, and agency. The wounded part of you needs to know that you will step up and say something whenever it is triggered and feels vulnerable, including using the boundary of saying no when you mean no.

Saying Yes When You Mean No

Recall a situation when a friend asked you to do something you didn't want to do. You didn't want to disappoint your friend, so you said yes, but inside you were screaming, *No, I don't want to do that!* The moment you said yes to your friend you went against your own boundary. You went against what you were thinking and feeling inside, what your authentic self actually wanted.

When we disregard and contradict ourselves, when what we feel inside and what we say and do outwardly don't match, we create a conflict. We violate and disrespect our own boundary. When you go against yourself and say yes but you want to say no, the only thing you have accomplished is momentarily avoiding an awkward situation. You avoided saying no and disappointing your friend. You avoided having to see their face sad with disappointment. You avoided feeling like you were a bad friend.

You had temporary relief, but the moment you said yes instead of honoring your no, you started a resentment cycle toward yourself, your friend, and the activity or event in general, and you may start dreading going at all in the future. If you went out with your friend anyway, you may have started beating up on yourself or feeling angry, and then afterward beat yourself up for having taken the time and spent the money to go. It is a vicious cycle, all because you didn't honor yourself and took the easy way out instead.

You avoided saying no at the beginning of this cycle because you didn't want to disappoint your friend, but you also let yourself down. You paid for your choice with resentment that you could have avoided if you had just said no. It would have been done, and you could have moved on. Yes, your friend might have been disappointed that you weren't going, but you would not have had to carry resentment over it. Resentment is heavy emotional baggage that is difficult to reconcile. You could have avoided this whole cycle by saying no. Easy to say, I know, but not so easy to do.

You pay whether you put a boundary on the front end or the back end. Either you put your boundary statement up front and pay the price of disappointing your friend, or you go along, not wanting to do whatever you said yes to, and pay the price with regret and resentment.

What if you don't want to do something but agree to it as an act of kindness or compassion? When this happens for me, I consciously acknowledge that I am going against my boundary system. I say to myself, *I know I don't want to do this, but I love her and want to help her out, and I know she really wants me to go with her.* Technically, this is going against my internal boundary agreement, but I am consciously overriding it to help my friend. I can't do that all the time, though, because if I did, I would quickly be back to a no-boundary situation and the resentment cycle would start back up.

What Happened to the "No" Muscle

You have always had the ability to say no. When you were a baby and didn't like something, you pushed it away, spit it out, started to cry, or did some other behavior to tell those within earshot that you were not happy. As a baby, you had perfectly intact physical boundaries. Something that came so naturally to you as an infant may now be difficult for you. Some lucky people learned healthy mental, emotional, physical, and sexual boundaries, but most of us did not.

> *Each time we do not state a boundary,*
> *we chip away at our sense of self-worth.*

So what happened to our "no" muscle? We learned to override it. We learned to be nice, to give in, to doubt ourselves, to put others first, to disrespect ourselves. We learned through a variety of interactions, methods, means, and wounded impulsiveness to override our natural gut reaction.

For example, if you told your mom or dad that your tummy hurt, your parent might have said, "You're fine. Go out and play." At that moment, your external boundary statement that you were not feeling well was invalidated. You learned to doubt yourself, to not trust yourself fully, and to question your internal boundary of how you actually felt. In that moment of overriding your gut reaction, your were learning to say to yourself that you can't trust your gut reaction, you can't trust yourself. When this invalidation happens repeatedly, the pattern of overriding the internal boundary begins. We know that the parent meant well, but they potentially set the stage for a lifetime of self-doubt in the child. This is how the wounding of invalidation and self-doubt begins, when the pattern becomes imprinted.

This invalidation reinforces the idea that the child doesn't have a protective voice. It confirms that the abuse or situation is going to happen no matter what the child does. This learned helplessness is then carried through to adulthood and can set up a pattern of abuse that is accepted in adult relationships. It sets the stage for seeing oneself as a victim. The lack of boundaries doesn't necessarily mean a person is a victim in their relationships, but there is a greater chance that they will not stand up for themselves.

When you contradict your inner voice, you say to yourself that you don't matter, that other people matter more, and that what they think of you is more important than what you think of yourself. When you do this, you are disrespecting yourself, violating your own internal boundary, and denying your feelings. You chip away at your own sense of self-esteem and self-worth. If you do this repeatedly over time, your sense of self becomes diminished, and your authentic self feels like it doesn't have a voice at all.

If you had a childhood of overriding or doubting yourself, your authentic self felt deeply invalidated by the time you were an adult. I have met with people who are so invalidated and so used to looking to another person to see what that person likes, needs, and wants that they have forgotten or don't know what they like and don't like. This is an extreme example, but you get the point that the more you go against yourself and say yes instead of honoring your inner voice by saying no, the more you lose your sense of self. Healthy boundaries are about honoring what your authentic self needs to embody to feel whole again.

Choosing Healthy Boundaries

Let's look at some specific healthy boundaries that you can start to practice right now. Start by reviewing your answers to "Exercise: Impulsive Reactions" in chapter 1. These are the wounded emotional tools you use. In the following list, find the items that best match to your impulsive reactions, then note the healthy boundary response that goes with each one. Pick one or two specific healthy boundaries that relate to your wounding, and start practicing.

- If you give away your power, the healthy response is to look at ways to pull it back in.
- If you say yes so that someone else won't be angry, then practice saying small no's. Let the other person feel their own feelings.
- If you try to control others, ask yourself what you don't trust. Then affirm: "I am in the flow of life, and I am my authentic self with others."
- If you try to manipulate others, ask yourself what you don't trust. Look at your internal boundaries.
- If you test others, ask yourself what parts of yourself you don't love. Say to yourself, *I am learning to love myself.*
- If you play the victim, ask yourself if it is for attention. What is this really about? Say to yourself, *I am learning to validate and accept all parts of myself.*
- If you overcompensate and keep doing for others, then look at ways to increase your self-love and just *be* instead of *do*. Say to yourself, *I am more than enough.*
- If you push someone away in the hope of starting anew with someone else instead of working on your relationship issues, ask yourself if this is a familiar pattern and if it is worth going through the cycle all over again.
- If you have low self-esteem, think of one thing a day you are proud of or that you did well, and express that to yourself.
- If you do not speak your truth, think of how you can honor yourself by speaking words that reflect who you are today.
- If you make yourself smaller to fit into someone else's world, gently stand up tall, take a deep breath, and know you are worthy of feeling your full power. Reclaim your worth.

Many of these healthy responses set and affirm internal boundaries. The internal boundary statements are what you say to yourself in quiet moments. You can work on replenishing your self-worth and self-love by practicing these statements, which will help to heal your wounded inner child and reinforce your boundary setting.

In chapter 4 we discussed broken and damaged boundary systems, where boundaries are not intact. In "Exercise: No Boundaries and/ or Enmeshment" in that chapter, you wrote in your notebook your responses to how your wounding shows up through weak or poor boundaries. Review those responses now. Are there any answers you would like to change now that you understand yourself better? Are these situations still happening in your life, or are things beginning to shift as you work through the HEAL process? Where do you need to establish or increase your boundary settings? What boundaries do you need to place so you can stop the recycled pain?

Once you are able to consistently set strong boundaries for yourself and others, you will begin to connect to your authentic self and have a feeling of emotional freedom.

When you are on your healing path and start to state your boundaries, you may receive pushback from others. This is normal. Your friends, family, and coworkers aren't used to hearing you express yourself or honoring your boundaries. They are not going to want the relationship dynamics to change; that is frightening to someone with poor boundaries. They will want to continue to ask if you want to do something, knowing they can talk you into it. In a way, you trained your friends that when you say no, it really means that they can convince you to say yes. Now you can stick to your no. Honor yourself and stand firm instead of giving in and making other people happy.

UNFORESEEN CONSEQUENCES

Setting boundaries where you haven't before can have unforeseen consequences. If you are brave and state a boundary but the boundary is ignored, rejected, or ridiculed, you will need to find a way to reinforce it. You need to defend your boundaries as if defending a castle filled with treasure. You have to be willing to go to any length to set and defend a boundary. A simple example is having a friend who repeatedly cancels on you after you make lunch plans. At some point you would probably want to set a boundary and stop making lunch plans with this person.

I had to set a boundary with a long-time friend of mine because I felt like I was doing all the work in the relationship. I was the one reaching out all the time, and the relationship did not feel balanced and reciprocal. I said to my friend that I was always the one reaching out and that his lack of reciprocity didn't feel respectful to me. My friend agreed and said that other people had given him similar feedback. He said, "That's just who I am, I guess." This was validating and disappointing at the same time. When I set my boundary (made my statement), he said he wasn't going to change, that that was who he was. I listened, and it was a turning point in the relationship. I am still connected to him and love him as a friend, but the relationship shifted.

> *When someone shows you who they are,*
> *believe them the first time.*
>
> —MAYA ANGELOU

To be clear, setting a boundary is not stating a threat or an ultimatum. It is about clearly communicating the consequences of another person continuing to disrespect you. Boundaries are not about control, because you have let go of the outcome. You are making your statement and waiting to see how they respond. Then you use your discernment to determine the next course of the relationship. When I made my statement to my friend about my feelings, I wasn't stating my boundaries to manipulate him, I was having an honest conversation about my feelings. His response told me what I needed to know to discern how our relationship needed to change.

RELAXING BUBBLE BOUNDARIES

Bubble boundaries, which we discussed in chapter 4, are boundaries set by people who want others to be close but not too close. Because of their boundary, attachment, and commitment issues, bubble-boundary people often have a push-pull aspect to their relationships because they never learned how to regulate their emotions. They grew up in an emotionally unavailable family household and have wounded emotional response tools such as low self-esteem, fear of change, fear of rejection, and perfectionism. These reactions are often the catalyst for the less-than language of *I'm not good enough*. (Note that someone who feels less-than didn't necessarily have emotionally unavailable parents, but this situation is an origin of this wounding pattern.)

This type of emotional wounding and lack of boundary knowledge and skill is demonstrated when a person pulls someone close, overshares, fears connection or rejection, and then pushes the other person away. This yo-yo interaction with others is exhausting and confusing for everyone involved. Bubble-boundary people dream of having a deep connection to others just like they wanted with their parents, but when others do come close, they push them away because they don't know what to do with the feeling or connection. They don't have the foundation of emotional attunement that is typically established within a childhood family.

People with bubble boundaries look like functional adults on the outside. They often have a good relationship and friends and a good job, but inside they feel lonely, isolated, and scared. They don't understand this because they think, *I should be happy. I have all of this in my life, but I feel closed off from everyone even when I'm surrounded by people who love me. I want to feel closer to others, but I just don't know how.* Their internal and external boundary systems are all out of whack. One minute they think they know themselves, and the next they are perplexed.

This overdeveloped, overgeneralized protection system prevents them from feeling connected to others, and being emotionally vulnerable with other people is difficult. They will mimic aspects of emotional intimacy with others, but this only goes so deep, as they have their bubble in stealth mode, waiting for any perceived attack. It is not healthy to be emotionally shut off from parts of the self and others, but the child didn't learn these skills, so it reenacts the wounding from childhood.

Story: Jessica and Her Double Layer of Protection

Jessica, a forty-three-year-old single woman, was doing a good job at working through her emotional wounding. She had relaxed her bubble boundary and was working on healing, saying affirmations, and setting boundaries. Yet with all of this work she still felt closed off, and her relationships weren't changing. As she continued to do her work, she began to realize that she not only had an outer bubble of protection but had also created an internal suit of armor as a backup.

Jessica had just gotten out of an emotionally abusive relationship and was internally well-defended with many layers to protect her emotional core. Even though she was out of the abusive relationship, the wounded part of her held on to this internal armor. She found that she could be vulnerable within herself, and she gave herself permission to enter into a safe, intimate relationship with her new partner, but she could only go so far.

Even though Jessica was working on healing her wounding, she hadn't realized what was holding her back from going deeper in intimacy until she discovered this internal layer of emotional armor. The deeply wounded part of her had held on to this armor because this part of her was hypervigilant and guarded, always looking out for the next emotional threat.

Through developing stronger and more functional internal and external boundaries, Jessica was able to know how she was feeling inside. She learned to recognize the resistance and evaluate it to determine if it was from her wounding or an irrational fear. Once she could do this, she was able to speak her truth, set her boundaries, and allow herself to become more intimate with her new partner.

The path to healing and embracing an authentic life for someone with all of these layers of protection is about understanding the wounding—what it looks, sounds, and feels like. As you have learned, a big part of healing is about understanding your role in your family of origin and discerning the difference between your parents' emotional baggage and who you authentically are. Much of the work that the bubble-boundary person needs to do is discerning that difference and then figuring out how to walk out of that maze. The exercises throughout the HEAL process are helping you to develop a clear sense of where your wounding and boundary deficits are, and to help you lay out a blueprint for the healing path.

Affirm strong and positive messages for yourself.
You are stronger than you think.

If you have a bubble boundary, where you want people close but keep them at arm's length, you may think you are protecting yourself. However, in your adult relationships, this protection shows up as avoidance, isolation, feelings of rejection, anxiety, loneliness, victimhood, confusion, perfection, feeling less-than, and shutting out others.

The following exercise can give you perspective on how your bubble boundary affects your relationships and how you can create deeper connections.

EXERCISE: BUBBLE WITH A WINDOW

This exercise will help you to evaluate your layers of protection and see how you keep yourself safe inside your bubble and keep others out. You can start building deeper connections with others by opening a window in your bubble.

Look back to your answers from "Exercise: Your Impulsive Reactions" in chapter 1. These wounded emotional response tools reveal where you need a better sense of internal and external boundaries. This exercise is designed to help you recognize what you are doing when you are doing it so you can gain new perspective on yourself.

In your notebook, draw a large circle in the center of the page that represents your bubble boundary. The inside of the bubble is how you feel and what you say to yourself, and the outside is your interactions with others, what you say and how you behave. Your bubble has a window that opens to your outside world. You can connect with others through this window, but it is also how you lock them out. As you go through this exercise, you will look at when, where, and why you want connection with others and when you shut them out.

Inside the bubble, write down what you tell yourself that keeps the window closed and you isolated. These are the reasons you have the bubble boundary, the purpose it serves. For example, you might list feelings of being scared, frightened, hurt, lonely, and confused. You might write your thoughts and actions that reinforce a victim narrative, such as *I'm not good enough*, *It's not worth it*, *I'm never going to find anyone*, and *I'm always rejected*. Perhaps you promise to give up trying to find a partner, believe that deeply connecting with someone else is too risky, or are tired of being vulnerable with others because they don't share anything with you. Or maybe you blame others, feel victimized, or are tired of the rejection. You can also write feeling words or expressions that you say to yourself over and over. (See the Feelings Chart in appendix A for feeling words.)

Everything you put outside the bubble either expands and connects you or contracts and isolates you. At the top and outside of the bubble, write down what your interactions look like when the window is *open* and you are connected to others. How do you interact? What do you say? These are actions and things you say when you feel safe and trusting of others enough to reach outside your bubble. Write down the qualities of what it takes for you to trust and connect to others, such as, *I can be myself around my good friends, I trust this type of person*, and *I feel safe when I go to this person's house or this kind of gathering*. This expands you and opens you up to bring others into your life.

Next, at the bottom and outside of the bubble, write down what your interactions look like when the window is *closed*. These are the actions you take and what you say to keep people at arm's length.

Do you avoid situations in which you have to talk with others? Do you only talk to "safe" people? Do you give people mixed messages? Are you noncommittal by using phrases such as, "I don't know if I can, let me see," or "Maybe"? Do you say you will do something and then back out at the last minute? How does your wounding and bubble boundary show up in your relationships? You can also write down people, places, and situations you avoid because they are too much work or they scare you. These words or actions contract and limit you, and reinforce that others should stay away, keeping you isolated.

Once you have identified how you behave and think outside and inside your bubble, ask yourself the following questions. Write down your answers to the relevant questions in your notebook.

- Do I still need to say these things to others to keep myself safe?
- What purpose does my bubble boundary serve? Do I just keep it out of habit?
- Am I truly unsafe in my connections with others, or am I overgeneralizing and unsure of my next steps?
- Do I keep people out of my bubble because I am afraid and don't want to be hurt again?
- Am I ready to welcome people into my life, or do I want to keep shutting them out?
- Do I still need to say these mean things to myself? How does this help me?
- What do I need to do to heal the negative messages I tell myself?
- What do I think is going to happen if I learn to set healthy boundaries and have my bubble window open more?
- How do these messages relate to my age of wounding? Is this a new age of wounding showing up?
- Do I give myself or others mixed messages?

- What do I say to others that gives them the impression that I want to stay inside my bubble?
- How do I feel when I look at the people and situations I trust when my bubble window is open?
- How do I feel when I look at the people and situations I don't trust when my bubble window is closed?
- Why do I close my window and not let others in?
- How can I get clarity with my boundary setting with others so I feel safer?
- How can I set better internal boundaries to be safe as an option to staying isolated?
- Once I am clear with my internal boundaries, what are some small steps I can take to open myself up to others?

Understanding why and how you keep others out when you really want to feel closeness will help you discern what you want to do with your bubble boundary. You have a choice in how you interact with yourself and life. You don't have to continue to keep other people out as a form of protection. This is not about popping your bubble and not having any protection; learning to set healthy, functional boundaries can replace your home-grown bubble boundary approach and help you feel authentically whole.

Setting Boundaries in Small Steps

Setting appropriate boundaries involves the current boundaries you have and the ones you need to develop. For example, you can try trusting someone by giving them a glimpse of the inner you, knowing there is emotional risk. As time passes, you will discern if they can emotionally hold your trust and personal information. They will either show worthiness or not through a variety of experiences, and you can go from there.

You can evaluate what kind of boundary you need to set if, say, a back-and-forth on your turn to pay for lunch turns into a small loan to a friend while they are unemployed—or not. Perhaps on a planned weekend getaway your friend is late and misses the flight. You are stuck feeling sad and hurt, and need to determine how to tell your friend what you are feeling. This is all good practice, with the importance on developing appropriate trust muscles and the ability to maintain emotional balance while events unfold.

A sign you are moving in the right direction is when you feel open to developing intimacy, connection, and life-enriching experiences that are separate from the actual outcomes. Outcomes will vary; the process and practice of appropriate openness is the key. Trusting yourself and your gut reaction of how you feel in each encounter will help you develop your boundary muscle. You will know when a situation feels right or not, and you will know what kind of boundary you need to establish. Your boundaries are always with you; you are learning what the correct boundary tool to use for the interaction is.

As you learn about boundaries, examine where your boundaries are strong and functional and where they need some reinforcement. Create goals for how you want to interact with others using strong internal and external boundary systems. Work from where you are to the goal, step by step.

Take an inventory of your relationships, and determine one person whom you trust and have wanted to go to a deeper level with but have been afraid to. Think about what you could share about yourself that would be OK to share with this person. One way to prepare for such a conversation is to write a symbolic letter about what you want to say to them. You won't send the letter, but this exercise will get you ready to go a little deeper with your connection. Assessing the information you feel comfortable sharing is important, as you don't want to overshare and go too deep too fast. If you do, you may not feel good about the connection afterward. This practice will help you create internal boundaries of what feels OK to share and what you are not ready to share.

There are three levels of information about yourself that you control:

Public: You can share easily identifiable aspects of your life, such as your name, the town you live in, your age, and your occupation. Think of things someone would find on a social media search.

Personal: You can share personal details that you already share with trusted family, friends, and coworkers. These include specific aspects of yourself such as your address, phone number, birthday, favorite band, favorite color, and things you enjoy.

Private: You can share details that you want only close family and friends to know, such as your health status, relationship status, fears, and fantasies. This is information that only a handful of people in your life know about.

In your notebook, make a list of family, friends, and coworkers, and determine the level of communication you feel safe sharing with each person without overexposing yourself. Next to each person's name list the level of communication you have now, and then determine whether this connection feels OK as is or whether you would like to have a deeper level of communication. Most people who are open-hearted in their relationships are at the personal level of communication most of the time, and only sometimes share private information.

If you want to open your bubble window and deepen a relationship with another, choose someone who will receive this information with love and respect. (It could be the same person you wrote the symbolic letter to.) Don't make a big production of having this conversation. You could simply say, "I've been meaning to share something with you," or "I want to talk about something that is hard for me to say, but I want to share it with you." Chances are they probably want a deeper connection as well. With this approach you establish an internal boundary of what is OK and not OK to share with them, and you invite them to know you on a deeper level. You are communicating that you want to be more open with them and hope that they can share more openly with you. It is an invitation for a deeper connection, which is a basic need for most people.

Remember that you are responsible only for yourself and cannot control or change anyone else, so however they respond to your sharing is their choice. The most important part of this process is that you are giving yourself permission to break the cycle of being guarded with others when you don't need to be. You are giving yourself the opportunity to experience emotional freedom in your relationships. However the conversation turns out, congratulate yourself for using boundaries and functional ways of expressing yourself to share a part of yourself. You are learning how to open up. You are learning to become emotionally available to yourself and others.

PICKET FENCE BOUNDARIES

Healthy, functional boundaries =
a healthy, integrated self.

Let's carry this discussion of healthy boundaries even further by using the metaphor of a picket fence. A picket fence creates a physical boundary between properties, and everyone can clearly see which side of the fence each property is on. You can apply this metaphor to a boundary between you and someone else. Imagine a picket fence between you and another person. You can see each other over the fence and through the slats. If the other person were in trouble, you could even jump over this fence to help. The fence creates definition and clearly marks where their space is and where your space is.

The picket fence metaphor is simple, as this type of imagery creates a partition between people and a reminder of the need for healthy boundaries. Learning to create imaginary picket fences as boundaries in your relationships is one of the most mature and responsible actions your adult responsible self can do to care for the wounded parts of you. This boundary setting will help those parts to feel safe, because your responsible adult self is taking action internally and externally to protect that wounded inner child.

The metaphorical picket fence between you and another person is a way for you to remember that you can have boundaries by saying no when you feel that no. The picket fence also helps to remind you that just as you are on your own journey, the other person is on their journey, too. Respecting someone else's journey helps us to remember to stay on our side of the fence. It helps remind the codependent part of us that wants to fix, rescue, care-take, or control that it is not our job to run other people's lives or offer suggestions when we are not asked.

EXERCISE: DETERMINING YOUR BOUNDARY STATUS

For this exercise, sit quietly in a place where you won't be disturbed. Have your notebook handy.

Picture yourself standing with someone you know. This could be someone you have a challenging time with or feel resentments toward. Now, in your mind's eye, see a picket fence between the two of you. Notice how you feel with the fence there. After you have had a few minutes to let your feelings arise, write down the answers to the following questions:

- With the picket fence in place, does the relationship between you and this other person feel different from the usual?
- Do you feel safer with the fence in place?
- Do you feel safer with that person?
- Do you feel separate from them?
- Do you feel distant from them?
- Do you feel it may be easier to speak your truth and set a boundary with the fence there?
- With the picket fence in place, what is the boundary statement you want to make to the other person?
- Do you feel like you want to tear the fence down so you can be close to them?
- Are you tempted to make the fence larger and reinforced?
- Do you have a more balanced sense of self with the fence between you?

Your reaction to this picket fence boundary can tell you more about your boundary status with this person and whether you need to adjust your boundaries with them. If the picket fence imagery helps you feel safer, this would be a good thing to remember as you are learning to set boundaries. If you want the fence to be higher or more solid, ask yourself what is happening emotionally. What reaction are you having that you feel you need a bigger wall instead of creating healthier boundary statements? Often we feel the need to have a bigger wall when others talk over us or don't listen to us. This isn't about a wall, it is about a lack of respect within the relationship.

If the wounded part of you rejoices when you build a picket fence, then it is feeling safe and the picket fence is serving its purpose. If you want to tear the fence down so you can be closer to the other person, ask yourself if this is a healthy relationship with healthy boundaries or if the picket fence feels too cold and unfeeling. Do you feel that the picket fence keeps you separate from this person or that it prevents you from loving and caring for them? These reactions are normal. Remember, you can still reach over the fence and give them a hug, so this boundary is not about not loving or caring for them.

If you feel emotionally safer on your side of the picket fence, think about what that tells you about your relationship with this person. Such a reaction means that you may need to evaluate and establish better boundaries with them. If you didn't have good boundaries with them before but the picket fence helps you to feel emotionally safer, you probably need to stand up for yourself more with that person, to say no or to speak your mind in general.

Repeat the exercise for other people in your life to help you establish your current boundary status.

PRACTICING DISCERNMENT

Learning to be quiet and still, to really listen to your feelings, is a key part of boundary setting. It is discerning how you really feel about a certain person or situation. It is determining whether you are trying to talk yourself into doing something, or if you are justifying or rationalizing your choices.

The more time you spend listening to and trusting yourself, the more you will be able to discern what is coming from you and what is coming from outside of you. If you are justifying a choice or telling yourself you "should," you are most likely doing it for someone else. The art of discernment is knowing what fits in your life today and what you have outgrown. Practicing daily discernment helps to clarify who you are at any given time and maintains an active connection with the authentic self.

Self-Coaching

You have learned that your responsible adult self is the part of you that steps up and sets appropriate boundaries, the part that will help the wounded part heal. Your responsible adult self is not just about helping the wounded parts, however; it is also the strong, steady part that is a champion for all parts of you.

The only way your wounded part is going to be able to heal and integrate is for your responsible self to establish boundaries, so you need to become your own supportive coach through this process. Now is the time to give yourself encouraging, reassuring, and loving comments to support establishing a connection with the younger self that carries the wounding. Begin to own your choices.

The following are examples of affirmations for supportive self-coaching to build self-esteem:

- I know this is hard, but I can do it.
- I am feeling stronger in myself every day, and I am worth it.
- I am trying my best, and I am proud of my efforts.
- Every day I am learning to set boundaries so I feel safe in my world.
- I am learning who I am and who I am not.
- I have a right to have my own feelings.
- I deserve to be treated with love and respect.
- I trust how I feel, and I express myself clearly to others.

These affirmations are just a few examples of how you can reassure yourself and affirm that everything you are doing is leading you to an expanded version of yourself. You may want to write down some supportive self-coaching comments that you need to give yourself at this point. This may be difficult if you are not used to using such language, but this kind and loving presence within will help to foster the gentle shifts that the HEAL process can create.

As you coach yourself through the process, you will begin to have greater clarity of what feels right to you and what doesn't fit anymore. This is when you begin to discern the voice or the feeling of your wounded parts as being different from that of your emotionally mature adult self.

Something else you must learn to discern is *carried feelings*. These are feelings brought from childhood that belong to someone else but are packed inside your toolbox because of what your parents or guardians modeled. Children pick up carried feelings of shame or fear, for example, especially if the household was chaotic or abusive. These feelings are carried into adult life, and determining whether the feeling is your own or not can be difficult. Most of the time, these feelings were emotions projected onto you that you absorbed into your sense of self, and you started to think that this is who you are.

Mark was a twenty-seven-year-old man who came to see me. His mom was always very anxious when he was a child. He learned from her to worry, to panic, to be anxious about thunderstorms, and to not trust others. He learned to carry her fear. When I asked him if this nervous, anxious way of being was how he wanted to think and react as an adult, he said, "Absolutely not!" Mark was anxiously overreacting to events in ways that a functional adult would not. He worked on recognizing the carried feelings that he had picked up from his mom. He learned to discern the difference between his emotions and his mother's. I helped him to develop a new internal boundary protocol—new functional tools—to use when he encountered situations that previously would have made him very jittery.

In her book *Facing Codependence*, Pia Mellody writes that one way to tell the difference between carried feelings and your own healthy feelings is that carried feelings are overwhelming, while your own, even though they may be intense, are not.[2] Carried feelings are usually exaggerated.

When you work on setting healthy internal boundaries, you get a sense of how you feel about something, and then you can discern how to react. In other words, you can choose how you want to react instead of how someone else would react. For example, Mark had learned to carry a fear of thunderstorms, but that was his mom's fear, not his own. His overreaction to thunderstorms was out of proportion to how a functional adult would response to a natural event. Once he saw that the fear was his mom's and not his, he was able to choose a different reaction.

When you work on discernment, you become clear about and have a healthy connection to what you think, feel, and choose as a functional adult. If your feelings become clouded, confused, or heavy, look at the situation and ask yourself if your wounding is getting triggered, what your boundary status is with that person, what you should own, and what is theirs to own. This isn't a hard and fast rule, but it may help you to discern these feelings as you integrate your wounded inner child with your adult protective self.

Setting healthy boundaries is one of the most important things you can do on your path to healing. You really can learn to create safe and healthy boundaries with others and to stop the pattern of having

2.   Pia Mellody, *Facing Codependence: What It Is, Where It Comes from, How It Sabotages Our Lives*, HarperCollins, New York, 2003.

no boundaries, being enmeshed, using bubble boundaries, or setting extreme boundaries.

Do the exercises in this chapter as often as you feel you need to, in order to understand your boundary system status and how to move it toward healthy patterns. You are well on your way to healing and embracing an authentic life.

CHAPTER 7

The Responsible Adult Self Steps Up

"By connecting your inner child to your internal being,
you bring out the hero in you that is inside all of us."

—KIM HA CAMPBELL, INNER PEACE OUTER ABUNDANCE

You have come a long way in your healing process. You have been working the exercises and practicing setting healthy boundaries. You are now ready to fully embrace your authentic self as your mature, responsible adult self takes charge of your life. There is more work to be done, of course, and we will discuss the final steps in your process of healing in this chapter.

Now that you have become familiar with your childhood woundings and the triggers you react to in your adult life, you may wonder how you can know the difference between the wounded part and your responsible adult self. The difference is in how you feel inside and how you react to situations. Your wounded self will choose, feel, and express in the following ways:

- Scared
- Victimized

- Blaming
- Resentful
- Uncertain
- Reactive
- Unaware
- Wary
- Confused
- Bewildered
- Wanting to avoid and hide

Your responsible adult self will choose, feel, and express in the following ways:

- Feeling solid
- Owning your life choices
- Practicing kindness toward self and others
- Being confident even when you don't know everything
- Being authentic
- Knowing who you are and who you are not
- Practicing self-control
- Being honest with yourself
- Accepting yourself and others
- Knowing when you are clear-headed and when you are distorting your truth

Your responsible adult self is like an internal kind, loving, and protective big brother or sister. It is the best of you, the part that you can count on to do the right thing, to show up.

The more you set boundaries, the more your wounded parts know and understand that the responsible adult self is going to be protective. The wounded parts will not let go of these wounded emotional response tools, no matter how destructive and dysfunctional they are, until the responsible adult self is able to consistently and confidently set internal and external boundaries. The wounded part is watching to see how, when, why, and where the responsible adult self addresses the situation any time a wounding is triggered.

> *If you are not respecting my boundaries,*
> *you are not respecting me.*

If the responsible adult self does not consistently come in and protect the wounded parts, the wounded parts will just stay frozen and stuck. There is too great a risk to let the defensive guard down because the wounded part does not want to get hurt again.

The following are various ways you can foster the responsible adult self to show up:

- Maintain consistent grounded and functional responses to triggers.
- Have a clear sense of ownership on whether you are making a choice or not.
- Maintain a clear and open channel with your authentic self.
- Practice kind, loving, and respectful affirmations with yourself each day.
- Discern what feels right and what feels wrong.
- Have a clear and assertive way of addressing boundary violations.
- Know where, when, and how to look out for all parts of yourself in a functional way.
- Know how you want to show up for yourself.

Your responsible adult self utilizes the functional response tools you developed as a child and as an adult. How has your responsible adult self shown up for you in the past? How does it show up now?

The following is a list of functional response tools that you may have brought into adulthood:

- Showing up for others
- Asking for what you need
- Loving yourself
- Loving others
- Practicing active gratitude with yourself and others
- Listening to your needs
- Hearing others, not just listening
- Respecting others when they speak their truth, even when you don't understand it
- Respecting the feelings of others, even when you don't understand them
- Being vulnerable with others whom you trust
- Sharing
- Being kind
- Offering to help others with no expectation of reciprocation
- Practicing gratitude
- Being proud of yourself, with humility
- Having selfless pride in others
- Finding courage when you are afraid
- Practicing loving detachment in relationships when needed
- Giving yourself permission to be vulnerable in relationships
- Learning to let go of feelings of shame
- Learning from others with humility
- Trusting in yourself

By taking responsibility for yourself, you own your life choices. You stop using your wounded emotional response tools and create functional tools.

Take some time to write in your notebook some examples of when you have seen others bring forth their responsible adult self and show compassion. For example, a buddy stepped up to help a friend, or someone brought kindness and compassion to another in need. Acts of compassion are great examples of bringing forth our most functional selves because they come from a place of selflessness, humility, and generosity. We aren't looking for anything in return, and only wish the best for the other person.

Now write down some examples that you have seen of someone being the bigger person, taking care of an issue, or owning a mistake. You can also write down some aspects and qualities of the functional adult you aspire to embody. For example, recognizing when things are too much and asking for help, or being vulnerable and sharing with a friend when you are sad. Being a functional adult doesn't mean we have to be strong all the time and never show what some perceive as weakness. It means being true to all parts of ourselves and working toward wholeness and integration. These are qualities that you may not be able to fully demonstrate at present, but are within your intention to achieve.

Keep your notebook with these qualities of the responsible adult self that you have described, and look back on it in a few years to see if the intention that you have put forth for yourself has manifested.

Learning to Say No

In the previous chapter we discussed the problems with saying yes when you mean no. Some people have a very hard time saying no because they don't want to disappoint, or they want to be liked and loved so much that they say yes to everything. This lack of boundary also comes from their wounded part being afraid and getting big and loud. Even the responsible adult can give in to the fear of not wanting to be left out.

The reality is, we all want to be liked and loved. I believe it is a core tenet of human nature. However, even when you say the no that is hard to say, you can still be liked and loved. In fact, many people are surprised when their friends and family begin to respect them more. We all have a deep respect for others when we recognize that they are standing up for themselves and what they believe in, and expressing what they need. Showing that vulnerability takes courage.

> *The ability to set boundaries directly corresponds to how much you have healed your wounded parts.*

As you work on setting boundaries, notice when and how the wounded self tries to go back to familiar behaviors of no boundaries or extreme boundaries. See this attempt as coming from the part of you that feels insecure and afraid.

Gently guide yourself to courageously use affirming language, and start out with some small no's. A small no could be someone asking if you want to have Italian food when you want Mexican food. Just state your no and your preference. This is not a do-or-die situation, but it will get you started. Setting boundaries is like using a muscle that is not used to being used. Start with the small no's and build up your strength.

The following are common misconceptions you may have when you begin to set boundaries:

- If I tell people how I feel, they won't like me.
- If I put myself out there emotionally, I am going to be hurt by someone.
- I don't want other people to see me as angry or mean.
- If I put a boundary statement out there, I have to live with it for life.

- I am not a selfish person, and boundaries restrict my caring nature.

Standing up for yourself may not feel natural at first, and might even feel forced. This is normal, and getting used to exercising this muscle is going to take a while.

Let's begin to exercise your "no" muscle. Recall a situation when you said yes instead of honoring your no. Now suspend judgment and ask yourself why you made that choice. What were you avoiding, or what were you afraid of? You will probably come up with some fairly good reasons why you agreed to say yes and didn't use your no muscle. In fact, you could probably convince yourself that you made the right choice by saying yes. If the choice you made was indeed the right and logical choice and you did it for your friend because such and such, then why are you carrying a smidge of resentment about saying yes instead of no?

The reality is that our analytical minds know our games and will talk us into making choices and saying yes when we want to say no. Our minds play tricks with our emotional selves, our authentic selves. This is because we have had a lifetime of training our minds to override our authentic selves and our boundaries. We have been socialized for all the reasons that I just mentioned and more to believe that we should say yes.

Recall again the situation when you said yes instead of no. Do you still think it was the best choice for you to have made to honor your authentic self? You may still say yes, and that's OK. The point is to ask yourself what your gut says the next time.

Suppose you have been asked to do something and you want to say no, but you are afraid to have the conversation because you don't know how it will turn out. I have heard people plot out a conversation like a chess match, develop a strategy for what to say, and then anticipate what the other person will say. I see this especially often with smart people who have control or trust issues. They know how the other person usually responds, so they plan to manipulate the conversation to go their way. They want to manage the conversation to get the outcome they want and avoid topics that are uncomfortable or unpredictable.

This fear strategy comes from the wounded self, which thinks that this is the way to set a boundary or have a conversation. It is not. It is manipulative, and the other person is going to feel this. It also denies the adult self the opportunity to be present and available to see how the conversation would turn out if the person used clear and assertive communication instead of being manipulative and indirect.

Many people have these strategic or managed conversations thinking they are making progress and setting boundaries, but they are only getting better at relationship chess, closing their heart, and failing in the relationship.

SPEAKING YOUR TRUTH

Many people who are just beginning to set boundaries want to be the "nice guy" and are afraid that if they say what they feel, they will be perceived as mean. This is normal when you are first establishing boundaries, as is feeling doubt, guilt, and perceiving yourself as uncaring or angry. These feelings go back to wanting to be liked and loved; we all want that, but not everyone is going to like what we say, and that is normal, too. Speaking up for yourself and speaking your truth can be done with kindness and compassion. You don't have to yell or stomp your feet to be heard; all you have to do is be clear and assertive in your delivery.

People often don't give others enough credit for being able to handle the truth. The feeling is that if we were to tell someone how we really feel, that person would crumble, break down, freak out, or get angry. The reality is that most people are resilient and able to handle unpleasant news or information. By not speaking your truth, you are implying you don't think someone is able to deal with it, so you are making a decision for them instead of respecting their intelligence and capacity for understanding. You cheat yourself and the other person out of an experience that could expand the relationship and deepen the connection. You deny deeper connections when you withhold your truth. You may also be implying that you don't want to speak your truth because it is hard for you to hold that reality.

When you don't speak your truth, you are saying on a deeper level that you don't trust and respect yourself, and therefore others probably shouldn't trust and respect you, either. After decades of working on my own healing journey, I am far more interested in respecting myself and being respected by others than being liked. When we speak our truth, we are loving and respecting ourselves. When we do our healing work, we become less reliant on the opinions of others to shape our ideas of self.

EXERCISE: OLD BOUNDARY PATTERNS

In this exercise you will list some life choices you have made that honored yourself and some that did not. You will be looking at whether you honored your boundaries and stayed true to yourself or went against your boundaries and made a choice to make someone else happy.

Take out your notebook and draw a vertical line down the middle of a clean page. On the top of the left side write "Works for Me," and on the right side write "Works for Them." Now recall a time when you said either yes or no to a situation or invitation. Think of the outcome, how you felt about it, and who you chose that yes or no answer for. Write a short description of the situation in the appropriate column.

For example, suppose you put in the "Works for Me" column that you went to a school you really wanted to go to, and you were happy with your decision, and in the "Works for Them" column you dated or married the person your parents wanted you to. Write down as many examples—minor and major—as you can, and see if a pattern begins to develop.

Now look at the examples you wrote in the "Works for Me" column. What was going on in your life at that time? Why were you able to honor yourself and your boundaries? Was this a time in your life when you felt good about yourself, when you felt strong and balanced? You were able to embody the feelings of pride and honor from those times when you spoke your truth. All of your choices in the "Works for Me" column were made by your functional adult self.

Now look at the "Works for Them" column. Why do you think you compromised your boundaries for other people? Why do you think it was more important for you to do what they wanted instead of what you wanted? Have compassion for yourself as you look over these choices. Each day we make the best choices for ourselves based on our view of ourselves and the world. You made choices that satisfied others earlier in your life, when their happiness mattered more to you than your own. Your emotional wounding made the choices in the "Works for Them" column.

If you have more examples in the "Works for Them" column than in the "Works for Me" column, it simply means that you were doing more for others than for yourself in the past. It means that you compromised yourself to satisfy someone else instead of satisfying yourself and your needs in the past. It means you avoided confrontations on the front end, but you paid for this emotionally afterward.

Looking over our life choices is interesting because we can see patterns of how our past behaviors influenced our future choices. These patterns continue unless we work on healing our wounding. As a thought experiment, look at your "Works for Them" column and imagine what the outcome would have been if you had made a different choice. Imagine what would have been different if you had honored your boundary system and stood up for yourself and what you wanted. Would your life be different today? This is another way to look at the power of choice in our lives.

Each day, in every way, you are the creator of your life. When you honor your authentic self and speak your truth, you create the best possible opportunity for your healing growth.

Story: Chandler, an Addicted Young Man

Chandler is a forty-year-old man who was struggling with addiction while trying to be a good husband, father, and provider. He would be fine for a while, but then he would get triggered by a life event and find himself driving to his dealer's house for another fix. He said he didn't know why he kept wanting to use, because he deeply loved his life, his family, and his business.

Chandler had been in and out of rehab multiple times, and had even gone to prison when he was twenty-one for dealing drugs. He understood addiction and the addiction process, but in all of the work he did to try to stay sober and in recovery, he never looked at the emotional part of his addiction. He had a damaged boundary system, so he recognized that he was hurting himself, his wife, and his family, but he would justify his behavior and get lost in the addiction.

In our early work together, I asked Chandler how old he felt when he was out of control, impulsive, and wanted to escape and use. What age did that behavior remind him of? Immediately he said it reminded him of when he was a twenty-one-year-old kid. At twenty-one, he was not only using drugs but also selling them, and his life was out of control. He spent over three years in prison because of dealing drugs. His early twenties was a time of huge upheaval and turmoil.

Long after Chandler was released from prison, when he would get triggered by the stress of work, family, and finances, his younger wounded self enabled his addiction. That twenty-one-year-old part would step forward and make poor decisions. Once the drugs wore off, the adult self, the part of him that was trying to put his life back together, had to face the wreckage and start the clean-up.

Like many addicts, Chandler hated this cycle. Once he identified and reconnected with his twenty-one-year-old self he could not help but see this pattern. He developed specific coping skills and boundaries that eventually changed the course of the pattern. His eyes were opened to the fact that he didn't want this recycled pain anymore. Still, his emotional wounding kept trying to get his attention. He could clearly see when his twenty-one-year-old self felt out of control and used those wounded emotions and logic to "fix" a problem.

Chandler had to set internal boundaries to protect himself from further harm, to stop using drugs, and to help the younger wounded part mature emotionally. These boundaries had to make sense to him, and they had to come from him. He wasn't going to do something just because someone else said he should. Addiction is a personal journey that affects other people, so he had to learn how to make a commitment to himself first and then to others.

Chandler used coping skills, such as fishing and working hard to be a good provider, as a way to give back and provide for his family. These skills helped his stress, but he was probably overcompensating at work as a way to boost his esteem. He wasn't making a grounded commitment to himself. He pushed himself too hard and was burning out. He was trying to rehabilitate his sense of self-worth by throwing himself into his work and exhausting himself, but this was just another addiction—workaholism.

In his timeline review, Chandler saw himself as a guy with a chaotic family background who got caught up in selling drugs, got arrested, went to prison, met a wonderful young woman, and got married. He was able to look at his early wounding experiences and saw how they set the stage for him to lose himself in drugs. He was grateful for his wife, but he didn't see that he was the one who created his reality, that he was the one who had worked hard to provide for his family. He still saw himself as the guy who went to prison and got lucky when he got out. It was hard for him to see his resilience, authenticity, and greatness because he was still in survival mode. Our discussions about boundary setting were like a foreign language to him.

We talked about how he could make a commitment to himself because he was worth it, but he didn't see himself as worthy. He saw everyone else and the life he was making as worthy, but he was externalizing his own worth, which meant that he would *always* have to overwork and overcompensate. He held this value outside of himself, not inside.

Over time, Chandler saw how he alone had overcome his struggles, found a wonderful life partner, worked hard at his job, and had children for whom he was trying to give more than he'd had. He could see that he was the one who had created that transformation.

In learning boundaries, Chandler made a commitment to himself (internal boundary) that he wouldn't use drugs because of all he had to lose. He placed a picture of his boys in his truck and talked with his wife more often. He learned meditation techniques and went to twelve-step meetings. He made a commitment to himself to do the hard work in the ongoing process of recovery, one day at a time. He resisted the urge to drive to his dealer's house. He often stopped his truck on the side of the road and sobbed with the internal struggle of wanting to use and knowing all he could lose if he did. His responsible adult self was confused about why he wanted to use, as it would jeopardize everything he had created. His adult self felt out of control and ashamed and angry. He was trying so hard to keep it all together and make it all work. He was working hard at recovery for his family, but more and more he was learning how to honor and love himself.

Chandler began making boundary statements such as *I'm worth it*, *I'm not going to let them push me around at work*, and *I'm going to speak up for myself and protect all of me*. The boundary statements to his wife (external boundaries) were messages of what he was feeling that day and how he needed her to help him with some things. This helped him to stop trying to do it all and then later resent her.

He was learning to not only survive but to thrive emotionally and to set strong boundaries. He moved out of the mode of seeing himself only as a former prisoner who was just getting by or getting lucky. The fact that he had served time in prison had become a prison that he had carried within himself, but as he healed from the inside out and found his self-worth, that illusion began to dissolve and fade away.

I want to be clear that following the HEAL process did not address Chandler's addiction per se. He attended twelve-step meetings throughout our time together, and he has a sponsor. He will probably always feel the pull of his addiction and will always need to work on his recovery. The HEAL process helped him to consciously identify what was happening to him instead of him unconsciously making emotionally reactive choices. Addiction issues tend to diminish when there is a prolonged sense of improved self-esteem, humility, self-care, and surrender.

Now he is able to recognize what his feelings are telling him, what he needs to do about them, and how stay sober. He can have conscious talks with his younger wounded self, set strong boundaries, and coach himself through triggers and cravings to avoid using drugs. Through the HEAL process, he found his authentic self again. He reclaimed what had always been there but had been buried under an illusion.

Chandler now has clear plans in place for keeping his addicted self from using when his addiction gets triggered. This relapse prevention plan is separate from the process he used to heal his twenty-one-year-old wounded self. He will always need to work on his addiction recovery.

Today I call Chandler one of my heroes, and I mean it. I am proud of his work, and I marvel at his courage, his tenacity, and his story as a man who has reclaimed his power and his self-love.

Developing Functional Response Tools

You have been doing a lot of boundary work and learning much about your own boundary system. Learning to set healthy boundaries is a crucial part of the HEAL process. The boundary work that you are doing will help you craft new functional response tools that fit your life today. You have looked into your wounded toolbox and seen all of the well-worn tools and impulsive reactions that served you so well as a child. Honor them, and know that they are always there if you really need them. But now is the time to develop some new, specially designed tools that fit who and where you are in your life today.

Through this work, you have also seen examples of how you haven't always shown up in a good way for yourself or others, or how you have avoided people and situations. Now it is time to focus a kinder, gentler lens on yourself. As you continue to do this work, observe yourself, don't condemn yourself.

EXERCISE: DEVELOPING YOUR
NEW FUNCTIONAL TOOLS

This exercise will help you to develop some new functional emotional response tools by understanding that you are in control of your mind, your mind is not in control of you. What instructions will you give your mind on how you want to experience yourself?

At the top of a clean page in your notebook write the words, "Who do I want to be for myself?" At the top of the next page write, "How do I want to show up for others?"

Under the first heading, "Who do I want to be for myself?", write down how you *want to be* in your day-to-day life. You can write some positive intentions, goals you want to achieve, or how you want to give yourself instruction. Write down your higher ideals and goals.

The language you use is speaking to the part of you that is healing, so write in positive, present-tense language. Here are some examples of positive affirmations to encourage you to be emotionally available to yourself:

- I am kind and gentle with myself.
- I find the motivation to go to the gym.
- I am proud that I eat well and nourish my body.
- I practice gratitude for all that is in my life.
- I honor my journey in recovery every day.
- I state my internal boundaries to myself clearly and lovingly.
- I am responsible with my choices when I smoke or drink.
- I respect my sense of self and know what is good for me and what isn't.
- I am learning to be emotionally vulnerable with myself.
- I can say no to someone, own it, and not feel guilty.
- I wake up each day and find the positive in life.
- I put a smile on my face to remind myself that I am loved.
- I am bringing humility into my life so that I may accept and love all parts of me.

Write as much and for as long as you want.

On the second page, "How do I want to show up for others?", write down ideas of how you *want to show up* for others in your life. You may want to create some positive intentions for yourself. You may also want to think of some higher ideals for when you interact with others. Here are some examples of positive affirmations so you can be emotionally available for others:

- I recognize when I need to be with others and when I need some alone time.

- I am truly present with my partner or spouse.
- I make good choices about who I surround myself with.
- I practice compassion for others.
- I honor my boundaries and choose others who do the same.
- I state my boundaries with others clearly and assertively.
- I am learning to be emotionally vulnerable to others and to not see it as a weakness.
- I feel good about who I am in my relationships.
- I respect the feelings of others, even when they don't make sense to me.
- I feel respected, loved, and trusted in my connections with others.
- My relationships feel reciprocal and nurturing.
- I practice humility in my relationships.
- I am opening my heart to those with whom I feel safe.

Again, write as much and as long as you want.

The goals and ideals you wrote down in this exercise are not magic formulas that create immediate transformations or new situations in your life; they are ideals that you will begin to hold for yourself. Over time, they will help you to create new functional response tools. You are setting intentions for behaviors and actions that you want to pull toward yourself and simultaneously be drawn to. Intentional energy will help you to discern and create better boundaries so you will attract others to you who are emotionally healthy and have good boundaries. (You may want to refer back to this list in six months or a year to see if you are manifesting these positive affirmations in your life.)

Over time you will begin to see and feel the difference because you are a conscious creator of your world. You are no longer in the daydream; you are living your life present and available.

Using Your New Tools

Through the HEAL process you are learning how to be a conscious creator of your life, and setting boundaries is the biggest key you can use to unlock authentic freedom. You are moving out of being on autopilot and reacting. You now have some tools to determine your boundary status at any given time. You can check in and ask yourself how you feel about something and which choice you want to make. That is your internal boundary system at work. You can also ask how you feel and then decide what to say to another person. That is your external boundary system at work.

The other big key to living an authentic life is to use your new functional tools. Learning to set responsible healthy boundaries and using functional response tools are both crucial steps in healing and embracing an authentic life. Healthy boundaries allow you to respect your own needs, desires, and wants without sacrificing your relationship to others.

When you show the wounded part of you that you can responsibly handle situations that were triggering in the past and can set healthy boundaries, you show all parts of yourself that you can be trusted to make mature, responsible choices. Self-responsibility helps the wounded part of you to let go and trust the adult self to set good boundaries and protect all parts of you. This leads to the final healing goal of self-integration so you can embrace an authentic life.

Pressing the Reset Button

Developing and learning to use your new functional tools takes time and practice. As you create new ways of responding, you will use trial and error to get it right. Suppose you are talking with a friend and you say something that you instantly know sounds bad or is not what you mean. Right at that moment you can press a "reset" button and correct the error.

When you realize you have said something that was not how you meant it to be, just stop, take a breath, and say, "I am sorry, I didn't mean to say that. I meant to say . . ." You can press that reset button right away and have a do-over. This is a highly functional tool to use, especially when you are practicing new boundaries and behaviors. It immediately resets the conversation and brings a new dynamic into your communication. You are saying that you are trying to be intentional and respectful with your language.

I often teach this tool to couples who come to see me. In intimate relationships we develop a shorthand way of communicating that is fast and quick, and we are often so familiar with the other person that we just blurt out what we want to say. This can cause problems to come up in the relationship. By using the reset button, you can immediately, or soon after, have a do-over moment and clear up any misconceptions or hurt feelings.

You can apply the idea of the reset button to many areas of your life. There is no need to walk away from a conversation and immediately beat up on yourself for something you said or did that was mean-spirited. Turn around, own your truth, apologize if needed, and say in a clear, grounded way what you mean. It is not hard; it just takes courage to be vulnerable.

In time, using the reset button will help you become more consciously aware of the choices and responses you have with others. It will help you to slow down, to not use your short-hand communication, and to be more respectful.

Shifting Perspective

Shifting your perspective to see how situations in your life can look different is a healthy and useful tool to help transform your life. Take a moment to look at the areas of your life where there is pain or unease. Ask yourself what is needed and what is in your control that can make this situation better. You can't change things out of your control, but you can change how you act and interact in situations. You do have power over your mind and what you do with your feelings. You can choose a more functional way to approach a situation.

Take out your notebook and find a clean page. At the top of the page, write, "Things I Would Like to Transform in My Life." Write down some situations in your life that you would like to change. Below each statement, brainstorm what you would change about the situation if you had a magic wand. As you review each item, ask yourself if there is an impulsive tool that stands in the way of your dreams. Is there something you believe or are doing that creates a roadblock for this transformation?

This exercise is just to help you see where you have power to change how you look at a situation and how you feel. So much of your healing work is simply about shifting your perspective.

In the next chapter you will learn how to integrate your inner child with your adult protective self, the final goal of the HEAL process. As you establish your boundaries and practice using your new functional tools, your healing child self is slowly joining with your responsible adult self and developing an awareness of people, situations, and context. You are exercising the emotional muscles needed to create this adaptive balance. The integration of the inner child with your responsible adult self allows for a richness in your life experience and opportunities for your expansive growth.

CHAPTER 8

Integrating the Wounded Child

The healed inner child becomes a source of vitality and creativity,
enabling us to find a new joy and energy in living.

—JOHN BRADSHAW

You will always remember what happened to you. Your experiences and timeline are yours alone, and your memories will always be with you, but you don't want them to be front and center anymore. As you have been working through this process, your inner wounding has slowly and deliberately begun to soften, heal, and transform, merging with your responsible adult self. Maybe you have already noticed how this wounding is becoming a footnote in your life instead of a chapter heading.

As you have been working through the HEAL process, you have probably discovered new insights about yourself. This is how you expand and grow into yourself. Through this process, you are learning to see and feel your known reality in a new way. You have the same life you had before you opened this book—probably the same job, same relationships, same friendships—but now you are learning how to look at your life through a different lens.

You may notice that the memories you put on your timeline are not as triggered or as raw as before. This is because you have found the courage to face these issues, to examine them, and to work through the hard feelings toward healing. You are facing things inside that you once felt were big and scary.

You may find that having this awareness is a gradual transformation, that you start to notice that you don't get as upset about certain issues that used to really bother you. Things are not as loud inside, and you are not as triggered by your wounded memories because you are healing that painful wounding. If this true for you, it means you have done a lot of hard work to heal and ease that pain. You are healing the familiar wounds you have had for so long.

How You Know You Are Healing

People often ask me how they will know when they are done with therapy. The short answer is, when your emotions are no longer triggered by certain situations. You will still remember what happened, but you won't emotionally react to it and feel "big" feelings. As a therapist, I see this as an indicator of a person's level of healing and whether or not they have worked through their wounding.

You may be creating safer connections, which allow you to feel free and open because of your new ability to set boundaries. It is easier to develop functional relationships now because you are paying more attention to yourself in the context of the connection instead of just reacting.

You are reconnecting with your authentic self, the calm and wise place that has always been inside of you. It was covered up by the illusions that others projected onto you and by your own misperceptions of situations. You are learning how to encourage positive self-talk and promote the authentic self to come forward and thrive.

Your wounded parts are putting down the wounded emotional response tools and impulsive reactions, and learning to trust your responsible adult self to be there.

Your wounded parts know and feel that your responsible adult self is setting functional boundaries. These parts don't feel as guarded as before and are loosening up.

Your wounded parts are no longer stranded and frozen in time. You are joining and integrating these parts with your responsible adult self.

You are no longer attracting wounded people into your life just so you can caretake, fix, or rescue them.

You're no longer getting into dysfunctional patterns with others by unconsciously playing out your emotional wounding with them.

If you are dating, you may notice that you are no longer attracted to the type of person you used to go for. You are able to consciously realize that this type of person wasn't good for you in many ways. Today you are making better choices and are attracted to people who have done their healing work. Healthy people find other healthy people.

Now that you are setting healthy boundaries, your wounded parts no longer have to do the job of fiercely protecting you. The wounded part no longer feels as hurt, confused, sad, lonely, and angry. Let this transformation wash over you as the old wounding dissolves away and your once-lost inner child integrates with your responsible adult self.

Trust is the union of intelligence and integrity.

—SOUMYA KRISTIN MATTIAS

All of these changes are your indicators that the wounded self is healing and integrating with your adult self. The wounded self has watched and listened for your responsible adult self to step forward, set boundaries, and protect all of you. Now it feels comfortable putting down the wounded tools because you are using your functional response tools to navigate your world.

The following are the ways you will know each day that the wounded self is integrating with your responsible adult self and that you are getting better:

- You feel a greater sense of freedom.
- You no longer become as triggered.
- You feel lighter and better.
- You are not as sad, hurt, and angry.
- You are in a state of connectedness and openness toward others.
- You feel like yourself again.
- You are kinder and gentler with yourself and others.
- You trust, love, and respect yourself more.
- You feel a sense of calm and wisdom.
- You feel like a thorn has been pulled out or that you have been released from captivity.

As you feel more integrated with your inner child, give yourself permission to attract others into your life who have strong boundaries and who are connected to their authentic selves. You may see how others set boundaries all the time that you hadn't noticed before. Practice saying the small no's, as this will strengthen your boundary muscle. When you are feeling brave and clear-headed, practice a bigger no. Remember that when you say no, in most cases you can say yes later if you want to. Be brave in protecting yourself with your boundaries. You are worth it.

You have probably been practicing making boundary statements in your head as you have worked through the chapters. If you haven't been stating them out loud when needed, now is the time to do so.

If a memory continues to recycle and you can't let it go, reassess the boundary statement around it, or create one now.

TRANSITIONS

Any time you go through a transition in life some parts are messy, and that is normal. Not everyone in your life is going to be on the same page as you. You now have an expanded awareness of yourself, your relationships, and how you fit into the world. This is your chance to objectively look at your relationships and ask if they are healthy for you and what you are getting out of them. This is when you realize you can be the creator, not just the reactor, of your life. Just remember that others in your life probably aren't going through this transformational process. They are on their own journey.

With this new perspective comes a shift in reality. You may feel disoriented about yourself and your relationships. You may not feel connected to your spouse, partner, or friends. You may start to question everything at this point, as things do not feel like they used to. You may feel like you are on the edge of a new beginning.

When you do this work, you are leaving one reality and stepping into a new one. You may long for your known reality, even though it wasn't always pleasant and relationships were toxic. Even with all of that, you may think *yes, it was a mess, but it was my mess.* Now you don't know what you are getting yourself into or where you are headed. It takes courage to be vulnerable. This sense of loss is a natural part of the process of unfolding, letting go, and claiming a new sense of self from the healing work. You have to shed this part of you to make room to heal and move on. You are learning how to give yourself permission to let go of the cycles you have been lost in for so much of your life.

You may start to see only the bad parts of your relationships and none of the good. You may see some things clearly and know what you need to do, and feel just as confused as ever with other situations. These symptoms are often confusing because you like how you feel and the progress you are making, but you don't see how anything is changing with others in their lives. That is because not everyone in your life is in therapy or going through this process. They don't have the perspective that you are developing. You are seeing yourself and your family and friends in a different way.

Lara was in a similar situation. She and I had been working on her wounded parts for a while, and she was doing fantastic work. She had gone through the steps and was having realizations about many parts of her life. She said that she was doing OK but felt sad, confused, and unsure about her next steps. She later revealed that she was going to stop therapy altogether because she didn't know what was going on and why she was having these mixed feelings. A part of her wanted to go back to her old reality, to pull out her old wounded tools and use them; at least they felt familiar. She said that even though she was learning new ways of relating to herself and her girlfriend, she was scared of the unknown.

I explained to Lara about this transition time and that it is common feel like this. We talked about the sense of loss that goes along with this work, as there is a grief component to this process that comes from a deep subconscious level. Lara had been in a bubble of the relationship dynamics with her girlfriend that she knew and understood, but now she was using her new functional response tools. She wasn't escaping into her old ways and decades-old wounded responses. She was out of the bubble now, exploring new parts of herself and interacting with her world differently. It was scary and exciting at the same time as she continued to develop stronger boundaries and more functional emotional responses.

Each time you revisit the HEAL process you will feel better and expand your awareness of yourself and your reality. You are on a journey from feeling emotionally closed and scattered to feeling free and open.

Bridging the Gaps

In your daily observation and discernment, you may notice that there are gaps in your life between having interactions that go well—when you are creating healthy, solid, strong connections—and when you go back to your old behaviors. This is a natural part of learning new skills; you are not going to be an expert right away. Gaps are the areas where you need to develop specific tools to use in a relationship or to consistently use the boundary tools you have developed.

Notice where you have safe connections, where the connection feels reciprocal, grounded, and nurturing. Now look at those areas where the connection feels uneven and you don't walk away feeling good about yourself or the connection. This is about observing your interactions with yourself and others and where you are using the tools you have learned. This isn't about judgment, it is about using your discernment to determine your role as a creator or a reactor. Notice where you are doing a good job at staying grounded and where there are some gaps in your functional response tools.

When things aren't going well in a relationship, you might think that you are not getting better, that the same things keep happening like before, and that the other person doesn't respect your boundaries no matter what you do. Or perhaps you are trying to set boundaries but are getting pushback, and then you stop trying. But feeling frustrated with the dysfunctional dance and really wanting things to change, you try again. This start-and-stop is normal when learning a new skill, but it can come across as a mixed message in a relationship.

If this is the case for you, you may need to reassess your emotional response tools. Are you still using some impulsive reactions that are familiar but not very functional? This is an opportunity to review chapter 4 and your responses to "Exercise: No Boundaries and/or Enmeshment." More importantly, though, don't think that something is wrong with your boundaries just because the other person doesn't respect them. This person may want to avoid the topic, not like what you are saying, or is narcissistically inclined. In any case, you may want to observe and evaluate the relationship.

When relationship dynamics are not changing and healing, you may be reluctant to set boundaries. It may be difficult for you to own your truth, or you may be indirect with your communication or scared that you may lose the relationship if you are honest. Perhaps you don't want to cause an argument and cringe at the idea of doing so. This avoidance is simply fear. You are stronger than you realize. Even if the relationship dynamics are not changing and things are not getting better, within yourself you are making more progress than you think.

When relationships aren't changing no matter how hard you try, look at what you can change and control, then evaluate whether or not the relationship is fulfilling to you. You may find that your relationships do change over time. This gradual process of reevaluating relationships happens over time because you are discerning what feels right to you, what is working, and what is going against you. You are learning to trust yourself and the process.

Relationships are always changing and shifting because they are dynamic. Gaps are going to occur even in established, solid, functional relationships. This is when you will need to check in with yourself, evaluate if something doesn't feel connected, and discern why you are not in attunement with someone else. Ask yourself what you can control or change in yourself without compromising your boundaries in order to make this connection more functional.

Remember, you are doing your healing work from the inside out.

Just because your outside world doesn't completely reflect how you feel inside doesn't mean you are doing something wrong. It means that you cannot control other people. You are living your authentic life, and in time you will attract and cultivate relationships that are fulfilling, reciprocal, and rewarding. Take ownership of your own life choices instead of looking for other people to change for your comfort.

As you do this healing work, the people with whom you are aligned and attuned will be there for you. Those who don't connect with who and what you are today will begin to drift away. Like attracts like. Your attunement will resonate with others who have done their healing work. You do not have to go through your contact list and cut people out. Connections and disconnections are going to happen naturally, and you will see who is able to grow with you and who is stuck in their own dysfunctional wounding.

Continue to observe yourself and others. Know that you now have the functional response tools to create positive outcomes for yourself. You want to be in the flow of your life, to stay grounded and consciously aware of the choices you make. You no longer have to react to life, you are your life's creator.

At the end of each day, take stock of your interactions with yourself and others. Notice where you did a good job with boundary setting and where there are gaps in your boundaries. Notice where you are doing a good job with your responses to others and where you need to practice using functional response tools. Notice where you are doing a good job encouraging yourself and where you are still beating up on yourself. Notice where you are expanding or contracting.

If you feel good about your interactions with others, then *congratulations.* You are honoring yourself and your relationships. If you still feel resentful or uneasy after an interaction, then reassess your role in the relationship and determine whether you need better internal boundaries or better external boundaries. This is not about perfection, it is about observation and gently guiding yourself to create good relationships with yourself and others.

You Have Come So Far

You have come a long way, far more than you realize. Think about everything you have learned about yourself and how far you have come. The understanding you have about yourself now is probably quite different from what you had when you began working through this process. You have given yourself permission to break down barriers and illusions about yourself, and are learning to look at and hold your hurt, pain, and fear. You are learning to create a sense of gentle closure within yourself for all of the wounding experiences from your childhood. You are being honest with yourself and your wounded past. The HEAL process has helped you to see how your once-hidden woundings kept resurfacing in indirect ways until you acknowledged this lost part of you and gave it a voice.

You were able to identify parts of your past that carried this wounding, and you helped it to clearly communicate feelings that were long buried but still felt. In doing, so you were able to rate the level of the pain, giving yourself a way to internally measure the intensity of the wounding.

You created a dialogue between the wounded parts and the adult part of you that didn't understand and couldn't see what was happening. This exchange opened up the communication so, that you could clearly know in real time how all parts of you are feeling and when these wounded parts show up in your day-to-day life. You have encouraged your responsible adult self, which has always been there but maybe in the background, to step forward and claim strength and agency.

Once you were able to reach through all of the pain and the

responsible adult self could hold that younger wounded part, then that part of you began to relax and trust that you were going to do your best to protect all of you. The boundaries that you employ will assist in reminding all parts of you that you can protect yourself in your personal relationships. These boundaries are the infrastructure that will keep you on course so that you can achieve your dreams and intentions.

Today your age of wounding is no longer lit up bright and flashing. It no longer gets triggered because you learned to listen to this wounding, heard its call, and addressed its needs. You are seeing what is right with you, not just what is wrong with you.

Don't let anything stand in the way of reclaiming your authentic self. Keep practicing your skills of boundary setting, owning and speaking your truth, and living your life as authentically as you can. Read over your earlier writing, notes, and answers to the exercises you did. Notice how you described events and situations at that time. Reread your healing letters. Ask yourself if you would describe those same events today in the same way, using the same feeling words. Do you have the same feelings about them now as you did when you wrote them? Or has your perspective shifted and you now have a wiser, calmer view of those experiences?

How have your relationships shifted? What patterns do you notice keep happening, and what parts can you control? Do you hear and see people differently now that you are growing and expanding? Notice how you may be drawn to people who are authentic, balanced, and happier instead of those who are drama-filled emotional vampires. Pay attention to these relationships, and listen to what your subconscious— your wise mind—tells you. Continue to trust your feelings and speak your truth so that you can live with a greater sense of freedom and love for yourself.

EMBRACING YOUR AUTHENTIC SELF

Your emotional wounding is no longer stuck in a snow globe wondering if there is a way out. You are well on your way to enjoying emotional freedom and embracing your authentic self. You are learning how to become your own best champion and how to be there for yourself in times of struggle and triumph. You are learning to hold and cherish those parts that once felt lost and abandoned and now feel integrated with and embraced by all of you.

You have learned new ways to reconnect and encourage that authentic, resilient part of you that was always there to come out and be full size again. You have learned how to honor your traumas and your triumphs because each has value, as all of you has value. You have learned that even though you are not perfect, you are perfectly imperfect, and there is no one else like you.

Your healing journey is going to have ripple effects throughout all of your relationships. By walking in your authentic truth, you will be showing others that you love, trust, and respect yourself. Others who are seeking this for themselves will be drawn to you because you have something they long for.

Because of your hard work, you will be able to authentically step up and be present and emotionally available to yourself and others. You will be able to claim your truth and speak with clarity, honoring yourself in all of your relationships. You will be able to name your wounded parts when they show up, greet them, and know what you need to do to heal them.

Feel the glow of self-love as it builds in you, filling in the cracks where you once held pain and sorrow. Let this wash over you like a healing balm that you have been yearning for all of your life. Feel your true, authentic self emerge and grow stronger day by day.

LIVING AN AUTHENTIC LIFE

You are learning to be a conscious creator of your life instead of reacting to the world, and you are now on your way to living an authentic life. As you have gone through the HEAL process, you have learned that having clarity is key to being able to see yourself through a healed lens.

One of the ways to keep this focus sharp is to develop some intentions for yourself. Intentions will help you stay strong and true to yourself and foster new beginnings on your path to becoming a creator and a manifestor. They will help you to discern that you are following your own path instead of blindly following someone else's.

Intentions are higher ideals or goals that speak to the part of you that is healing and seeking balance. These are the qualities of self that you want to embody, cherish, and aspire to. They are statements written in positive, present-tense language. The following are some intentions for you to refer to when you need a gentle reminder of your strength and wisdom:

- I am kind and gentle with myself.
- I love myself.
- I trust myself.
- I respect myself.
- I find the motivation to move my body.
- I am proud that I am eating well and nourishing my body.
- I respect my sense of self and know what is good for me and what isn't.
- I can say no to someone else, own it, and not feel guilty.
- Every day, in every way, I live my life to its fullest.
- My boundaries help me feel a sense of safety in my personal relationships.

- I make better choices about who I surround myself with on a daily basis.
- I feel good about who I am in my relationships with others.
- I feel respected, loved, and trusted by those in my life.
- My relationships nurture me and feel reciprocal.
- I bring others into my life who are emotionally healthy and create positive relationships.
- I am grateful that I continue to work on my relationship with myself because, in the end, I matter the most.
- I am proud of all of my hard work and my accomplishments.
- Today I am wiser than I ever thought I could become.

Use these intentions as a guide, and create your own intentions that match the aspirations you have for your authentic life. Some of your intentions may already be happening in your life. Using them will help you to continue developing new functional response tools. They will help you to discern and create better boundaries so that you can create functional, loving relationships with yourself and others.

The following are some messages I hope you can deeply feel and know within yourself. Read them aloud from the grounded place inside of you that holds your healed self and feels the self-love you are encouraging and growing each day.

I know each step of the way, and I respect all of the hard work that I have put into myself to get to this point on my authentic, resilient pathway. I am proud of my work.

I know the pain I felt when I touched my wounding and gave myself permission to be vulnerable to those feelings. I realize now how strong I am.

Having been hurt by words, I use my words to speak my gentle truth, to encourage, and to defend. I am worthy of speaking up for myself.

I know that I am stronger than I give myself credit for.

My accomplishments and experiences, large or small, all play a role in creating abundance in my life. I greet each day with hope, trust, and a sense of inner strength.

I know that I have healed my emotional wounding and the parts that I have worked on up to this point. Today and every day I am the best representation of me.

I know that I am a work in progress and that I probably have challenges waiting for me to heal, but right now I feel good about myself. I am enjoying the journey each day.

I feel a gentle closure with many of the wounding experiences from my childhood. I feel the satisfied sense of the hard work that brought me to this place.

I know that my relationship with myself and others is stronger today because of the work I have done within myself. I love myself.

I know that the ripple effects from my healing will touch all those whom I encounter. I am walking on my authentic path.

I know that I didn't get here alone, that all of those whom I have encountered on my journey have helped me to understand my strengths, courage, and vulnerabilities, and I am humbly grateful. I feel connected to those who love me for me.

I wish you many fulfilling days ahead as you bring your best self forward and love, trust, and respect yourself. You have come full circle. Your lost wounded parts are integrated with your responsible adult self. You are no longer lost or wounded. You have rejoined with your authentic self. Welcome home.

> At the end of your unraveling,
> you will look down and see your own feet
> that have carried you so, so far
> and you will decide for once that it is okay
> to sit down
> to rest
> to hold out your hands
> to lift up your head
> to open your heart
> to the possibility that you were never alone after all
> not for one minute
>
> That Love was right there
> in her terrible silence
> not quite sure how to say it so you would believe her
> that you were a thing of rare beauty on the earth
> That She still has your macaroni necklace
> That She's been following you around,
> making maps of all the places you've been lost,
> so you'd know how to get back when the time came
> to put it all to rest.[1]

---

1. Excerpted from "Love Will Find You Out" by Jen Lemen. Reprinted with permission.

Feelings Charts

These chart lists many words you can use to describe feelings, both emotional and physical. The words are divided in two categories: feelings we have when our needs are satisfied, and feelings we have when our needs are not met.

Look through the words when you want to express specific feelings so you can be clear when communicating your feelings.[2]

---

1. Feelings Chart reprinted by permission. (c) 2005 by Center for Non-violent Communication. Website: www.cnvc.org. Email: cnvc@cnvc.org. Phone: +1.505.244.4041.

Feelings when your needs are satisfied

AFFECTIONATE
compassionate
friendly
loving
open hearted
sympathetic
tender
warm

ENGAGED
absorbed
alert
curious
engrossed
enchanted
entranced
fascinated
interested
intrigued
involved
spellbound
stimulated

HOPEFUL
expectant
encouraged
optimistic

CONFIDENT
empowered
open
proud
safe
secure

EXCITED
amazed
animated
ardent
aroused
astonished
dazzled
eager
energetic
enthusiastic
giddy
invigorated
lively
passionate
surprised
vibrant

GRATEFUL
appreciative
moved
thankful
touched

INSPIRED
amazed
awed
wonder

JOYFUL
amused
delighted
glad
happy
jubilant
pleased
tickled

EXHILARATED
blissful
ecstatic
elated
enthralled
exuberant
radiant
rapturous
thrilled

PEACEFUL
calm
clear headed
comfortable
centered
content
equanimous
fulfilled
mellow
quiet
relaxed
relieved
satisfied
serene
still
tranquil
trusting

REFRESHED
enlivened
rejuvenated
renewed
rested
restored
revived

Feelings when your needs are not satisfied

AFRAID
apprehensive
dread
foreboding
frightened
mistrustful
panicked
petrified
scared
suspicious
terrified
wary
worried

ANNOYED
aggravated
dismayed
disgruntled
displeased
exasperated
frustrated
impatient
irritated
irked

ANGRY
enraged
furious
incensed
indignant
irate
livid
outraged
resentful

AVERSION
animosity
appalled
contempt
disgusted
dislike
hate
horrified
hostile
repulsed

CONFUSED
ambivalent
baffled
bewildered
dazed
hesitant
lost
mystified
perplexed
puzzled
torn

DISCONNECTED
alienated
aloof
apathetic
bored
cold
detached
distant
distracted
indifferent
numb
removed
uninterested
withdrawn

DISQUIET
agitated
alarmed
discombobulated
disconcerted
disturbed
perturbed
rattled
restless
shocked
startled
surprised
troubled
turbulent
turmoil
uncomfortable
uneasy
unnerved
unsettled
upset

EMBARRASSED
ashamed
chagrined
flustered
guilty
mortified
self-conscious

FATIGUE
beat
burnt out
depleted
exhausted
lethargic
listless
sleepy
tired
weary
worn out

PAIN
agony
anguished
bereaved
devastated
grief
heartbroken
hurt
lonely
miserable
regretful
remorseful

Feelings when your needs are not satisfied, cont.

SAD	TENSE	VULNERABLE	YEARNING
depressed	anxious	fragile	envious
dejected	cranky	guarded	jealous
despair	distressed	helpless	longing
despondent	distraught	insecure	nostalgic
disappointed	edgy	leery	pining
discouraged	fidgety	reserved	wistful
disheartened	frazzled	sensitive	
forlorn	irritable	shaky	
gloomy	jittery		
heavy hearted	nervous		
hopeless	overwhelmed		
melancholy	restless		
unhappy	stressed out		
wretched			

Needs Inventory

Needs are an essential part of our lives. They are different from wants, which are fleeting aspects that do not have lasting value. Needs fulfill our sense of self-worth and esteem at a deeply fundamental level. Identifying your needs will help you to understand yourself better, and you will be able to communicate your needs to others more clearly. Knowing your needs allows you to have a deeper connection to yourself.

Look over this chart to identify your needs that are being met right now and those you want to manifest.[1]

---

1. Reprinted by permission. (c) 2005 by Center for Nonviolent Communication. Website: www.cnvc.org Email: cnvc@cnvc.org. Phone: +1.505.244.4041

Needs Inventory

CONNECTION

acceptance
affection
appreciation
belonging
cooperation
communication
closeness
community
companionship
compassion
consideration
consistency
empathy
inclusion
intimacy
love
mutuality
nurturing
respect/self-respect

CONNECTION
continued

safety
security
stability
support
to know and
  be known
to see and be seen
to understand and
  be understood
trust
warmth

**PHYSICAL
WELL-BEING**

air
food
movement/exercise
rest/sleep
sexual expression
safety
shelter
touch
water

HONESTY

authenticity
integrity
presence

PLAY

joy
humor

PEACE

beauty
communion
ease
equality
harmony
inspiration
order

AUTONOMY

choice
freedom
independence
space
spontaneity

MEANING

awareness
celebration of life
challenge
clarity
competence
consciousness
contribution
creativity
discovery
efficacy
effectiveness
growth
hope
learning
mourning
participation
purpose
self-expression
stimulation
to matter
understanding

APPENDIX C

Resources

The following are resources to help you with a variety of needs.

National *Domestic Violence Hotline:* 1-800-799-7233,
www.thehotline.org

Look up your local resource in advance so you that understand your
rights for establishing a domestic violence restraining order, also
known as a temporary protective order, in the United States and
its territories.

The National *Suicide Prevention* Lifeline: 1-800-273-8255,

www.suicidepreventionlifeline.org

National Institute of Mental Health: www.nimh.nih.gov

Victories for Men: www.victoriesformen.org

The Art of Manliness: www.artofmanliness.com

Mental health support for active military, veterans and their families:

www.giveanhour.org

Alcoholics Anonymous: www.aa.org

Narcotics Anonymous: www.na.org

The Trevor Project for LGBT issues: 1-866-488-7386, www.thetrevorproject.org

Codependents Anonymous: www.coda.org

To access the companion workbook to *Healing Your Lost Inner Child* for additional material, shared stories, and in-depth exercises, please visit my website at www.theartofpracticalwisdom.com.

For further reading on the subject of inner child work and other personal work, the following books may be of interest to you:

Dr. Eric Berne: Games People Play: The Psychology of Human Relationships, Tantor Media, 2011

John Bradshaw: Homecoming: Reclaiming and Championing Your Inner Child, Bantam, 1992.

Dr. Brené Brown: *Daring Greatly: How the Courage to Be Vulnerable Transforms the Way We Live, Love, Parent, and Lead*, Avery, reprint ed., 2015.

Jeff Brown: *Love It Forward*, Enrealment Press, 2014.

Susan Cain: *Quiet: The Power of Introverts in a World That Can't Stop Talking*, Broadway Books, 2013.

Doris Eliana Cohen, PhD: *Repetition: Past Lives, Life, and Rebirth*, Hay House, Inc., 2008.

Panache Desai: *You Are Enough: Revealing the Soul to Discover Your Power, Potential, and Possibility*, HarperCollins, 2020.

Dr. Joe Dispenza: *Becoming Supernatural: How Common People Are Doing the Uncommon*, Hay House, Inc., 2017.

Matthew Fox: *The Hidden Spirituality of Men: Ten Metaphors to Awaken the Sacred Masculine*, New World Library, 2008.

Louise Hay: *You Can Heal Your Life,* Hay House, Inc., 1984.

Dr. Bessel van der Kolk: *The Body Keeps the Score: Brain, Mind, and Body in the Healing of Trauma*, Penguin Books, 2015.

Dalai Lama, Desmond Tutu, & Douglas Carlton Abrams: *The Book of Joy: Lasting Happiness in a Changing World*, Avery, 2016.

Jackson MacKenzie: *Whole Again: Healing Your Heart and Rediscovering Your True Self after Toxic Relationships and Emotional Abuse*, Penguin Random House, 2019.

Dr. Karyl McBride, PhD: *Will I Ever Be Good Enough?: Healing The Daughters of Narcissistic Mothers*, Atria Books, reprint ed., 2008.

Pia Mellody: *Facing Codependence: What It Is, Where It Comes From, How It Sabotages Our Lives*, HarperCollins, 1989.

Alice Miller: *The Drama of the Gifted Child: The Search for the True Self*, Basic Books, 2008.

Vivek H. Murthy, MD: *Together: The Healing Power of Human Connection in a Sometimes Lonely World*, HarperCollins, 2020.

Mark Nepo: *The Book of Awakening: Having the Life You Want by Being Present to the Life You Have*, Conari Press, 2000.

Michael Newton, PhD: *Destiny of Souls: New Case Studies of Life Between Lives*, Llewellyn Publications, 2000.

Michael Newton, PhD: *Journey of Souls: Case Studies of Life between Lives*, Llewellyn Publications, 5th ed., 2019.

Newton Institute: *Wisdom of Souls: Case Studies of Life between Lives from the Michael Newton Institute*, Llewellyn Publications, 2019.

Eleanor Payson: *The Wizard of Oz and Other Narcissists: Coping with One-Way Relationships in Work, Love, and Family*, Julian Day Publications, 3rd ed., 2002.

Terrence Real: *I Don't Want to Talk about It: Overcoming the Secret Legacy of Male Depression*, Scribner, reprint ed., 1999.

David Richo: *How to Be an Adult in Relationships: The Five Keys to Mindful Loving*, Shambhala Publications, 2002.

Ross Rosenberg: *The Human Magnet Syndrome: The Codependent Narcissist Trap*, Morgan James Publishing, 2019.

Babette Rothschild: *The Body Remembers: The Psychophysiology of Trauma and Trauma Treatment*, W. W. Norton & Company, 2000.

Gary Zukav: *The Seat of the Soul*, Fireside/Simon & Schuster, Inc., 1989.

Glossary

activated: An internal process whereby one is reminded of a memory via sight, sound, smell, or touch. The stimulus that initiates the memory recall and often leads to a change in one's mood or behavior. See also **triggers**.

age of wounding: The age at which an initial emotional wounding occurs, usually in childhood. An age representing a part that did not mature emotionally with the rest of one.

attuned/attunement: To resonate and connect emotionally with the inner world of another and reflect this back to them. To feel connected or aligned on a deep energetic and emotional level with another.

authenticity: To have a sense of freedom of self-expression. Congruence with how one feels inside with how one presents outside.

boundaries: A sense of where one person ends and another begins, which creates emotional safety in personal relationships. Established through words or actions.

boundary violation: A lack of respect or acknowledgment for a boundary that is implied or spoken. Boundary violations can come from oneself or from another person.

bubble boundary: A semi-permeable, flexible yet rigid boundary whereby one keeps another or others at arm's length emotionally. Simultaneously being guarded and open.

carried feelings: Feelings that were put on an individual by someone else, or feelings an individual picked up from another person thinking they were that individual's responsibility to hold. Often leads to having emotional overreactions.

childhood family: The family in which one was raised. Could be a birth family, an adopted family, a foster family, or a blended family.

codependent: Having a higher regard, esteem, love, trust, and respect for someone else than one has for oneself. The over-reliance on other people for a sense of self or validation of self.

core wounding: An emotional trauma that happens at one time or over the course of time that impacts sense of self, choices, and life outcomes.

discernment: Having clarity for what one likes and doesn't like. The ability to look through many elements to find that which rings true for an individual.

dissociate/dissociation: To internally disconnect or "escape" an abusive or traumatic situation or person by mentally departing from a present sensory and physical reality. Typically occurs during the trauma but can also occur afterward, in which the individual appears to be daydreaming or "spacing out."

emotions: A subjective state of mind that can be a reaction to an internal stimulus, such as a thought or memory, or a reaction to an external event. Can manifest both consciously or subconsciously.

emotional response tools: Generally developed in childhood, although learned throughout the lifespan. Such tools create a catalogue of reactions, behaviors, thoughts, and feelings toward a stimulus. Tools can be functional, as in helping an individual achieve their goals, or wounded, which work against the individual. Both types of emotional response tools are internally developed without initial conscious knowledge of which tools are "good" or "bad."

emotional standouts: Events from one's past that have a weighted impact on how one sees oneself and one's life. Memory experiences recalled without a lot of effort; can be of pain or great joy.

emotionally unavailable: The absence of knowing how to give or receive emotions within a relationship. Connection to feelings are shut down or ignored. The emotionally unavailable person does not recognize this deficit within themselves, nor do they realize when others need emotional validation and support. Usually passed down from one generation to the next until the cycle is healed.

enmeshment: To be so close to someone else, usually a family member, that one doesn't know where others begin and the individual ends. Found in dysfunctional family dynamics in which everyone is in everyone else's business and tells others what to do. Boundaries that are fuzzy, unclear, or utilized only part time.

explicit memories: Also known as declarative memories. The conscious retrieval and recollection of long-term memories consisting of experiences, ideas, and facts.

external boundaries: Statements or actions toward others that demonstrate and declare what is acceptable and unacceptable to an individual.

extreme boundary: Blocking, shutting down, "ghosting," leaving town, or putting up high emotional walls between oneself and another or others.

false self: An unconscious negative self-concept that usually originates in and is reinforced by the family of origin. An illusion that one is less-than, bad, defective, or broken.

feelings: Emotional states or reactions such as anger, joy, and sadness. The conscious experience of emotional reactions.

functional response tools: A response to a situation that comes from an authentic and grounded place. Usually a productive response that encourages better relationship dynamics and a more positive outcome. Developed throughout the lifespan.

grounded: To feel centered within oneself and solid about a thought, feeling, or response. A feeling or response that originates from a healed place, not from a place of pain.

healing letters: Symbolic letters of affection to one's younger self or adult self that express deep feelings of validation, love, and care. Written fast and furiously as an energy exchange coming from inside the individual. Such letters are not given, mailed, or shared; they are meant to be shredded or burned after writing. They create a dialogue to encourage the integration of the lost wounded parts of the self with the responsible adult self.

implicit memories: The use of past experiences to remember things without thinking about them. It does not require conscious retrieval; that is, a red light means stop and green means go.

impulsive reactions: Responding to a stimulus without much thought. A quick reaction that often does not come from a grounded place within but from a place of wounding or pain.

inner child: A concept a person envisions that holds the emotional imprinted memory from childhood. Can be authentic and emotionally unencumbered or wounded and traumatic. If wounded, it can be referred to as the wounded inner child or the lost inner child. A representation of one's younger self. Also referred to as a "part" or "parts" of someone.

integration: The dynamic process of joining the lost, wounded inner child with the functional and responsible adult self. A place of healing accomplished through introspection, self-reflection, and development of a greater perspective of one's life events and emotional landscape. A feeling of being whole, not fragmented or scattered.

internal boundaries: Commitments and agreements with oneself about what are acceptable and unacceptable thoughts, feelings, and behaviors one chooses for one's life and how one wants to express them.

magical thinking: To look at a solution or situation through a lens of fantasy or innocence that is not practical or realistic. A reactive response when not wanting to connect with reality and leaving out key details of exactly how something could be accomplished. A childlike response to a complex situation.

mind reading: Also known as fortune telling. Projecting onto someone else one's own fears, insecurities, and shortcomings. Making up falsehoods.

narrative: The story one embodies relating to who they are, what they are like, and what they feel they deserve. The story can be based on fact, falsehoods, or distorted beliefs of oneself.

needs: Basic necessities of life required for a functional survival: love, nurturing, food, shelter, clothing, and so on. More than just food and shelter, and not superfluous or a luxury. Needs fulfill a sense of self-worth and esteem at a deep fundamental level.

needless: The absence of asking or giving to oneself that which is necessary to live safely, comfortably, or able to have an emotionally fulfilling life. Through neglecting the needs of the self, the child develops and carries a false belief that they have no legitimate needs. By ignoring their needs in adulthood, such an individual does not have to face the painful reality that their basic needs were not met in childhood. Often originates from an emotionally unavailable household in which the child eventually stops asking for their needs to be met. This results in the adult having difficulty knowing how to make intimate connections with others because their basic emotional needs were neither met nor mirrored by their parents.

opposition: To be incongruent with another's opinion, belief, or behavior.

projection: A person's unconscious and unresolved emotional pain directed toward another, often in the form of finding fault in others. Identifying a wounding within someone else that is not healed within oneself and then shaming that person for one's own issues.

recycled pain: Feelings or memories that repeatedly come up and do not go away until acknowledged, validated, or healed.

resentment: A hurt feeling that continues to recycle and is hard to move past.

resilience: The ability to find the internal resources to respond to a situation. A source of strength and steadfastness deep within. The degree to which an individual can bounce back from a situation that occurs unexpectedly.

responsible adult self: A part of oneself that has matured emotionally and responds to a situation in a grounded and functional way. Sets and maintains boundaries for all parts of the self. A champion for all parts of the self.

self-attunement: The process of connecting with the self so that all parts of the self are congruent, balanced, and whole. To consciously know and be in alignment with the needs of the authentic self.

suppression: When an individual consciously tries to push a memory out of their awareness. Willing oneself to forget about something.

synergistic: The dynamic interaction and cooperation of persons, places, or things that creates something that is greater than any one of the parts. To feel connected on a deep level with another, resulting in an idea or feeling that cannot be achieved by someone on their own.

traumatic core wounding: A deep, profound emotional wounding that can be physical, mental, emotional, or sexual in nature. Takes longer to process and heal.

trigger/triggering event: A present-day situation, sight, sound, smell, or touch that activates a memory of a past event, usually traumatic. See also **activated**.

wants: A desire or wish to possess or experience something. That which is not needed but would be nice to have. That which is fleeting and not long-lasting.

wantless: To forego any idea of desire for someone or something else. Often seen in individuals who grew up in an emotionally unavailable household in which basic needs and wants were neglected or ignored. Wantless individuals do not know how to express what they like or do not like.

wounded emotional response tools: An emotional response tool that is rooted in a place of fear or pain within an individual and creates poor or dysfunctional lifelong relationship patterns. Developed throughout the lifespan.

wounded parts; wounded self; wounded, lost inner child: Terms that refer to the conscious and unconscious emotional aspects of oneself that are not healed and are often emotionally buried. Internal emotional wounds that are not seen or known to others but show up in indirect ways, such as passive-aggressiveness, self-sabotage, and patterns of making bad choices, often resulting in negative outcomes.

About the Author

ROBERT JACKMAN is a board certified Psychotherapist with the National Board of Certified Counselors who has helped many people on their healing path for more than twenty years. In addition to his private practice, he has taught master's level classes at National Louis University in the Chicago area, led outpatient groups in hospitals, given lectures on mindfulness, hypnotherapy, codependency, and the role of spirituality in healing, and participated in numerous weekend retreats with Victories for Men.

Robert is also a Reiki master who uses energy psychology in his practice and considers himself a codependent in recovery, always working on boundary setting, discernment and connecting with his authentic self. He lives in the far west suburbs of Chicago and in Oregon with his family. He enjoys photography, kayaking, gardening, and nurturing and delighting his inner child.

For more information about Robert Jackman, his other works, upcoming events and the *Healing Your Lost Inner Child* book and companion workbook, please visit www.theartofpracticalwisdom.com.

Made in the USA
Coppell, TX
10 November 2022